# A SINGLE WOMAN'S SASSY GUIDE

NOCTUA
MENTIS

Published in Australia by
Noctua Mentis
Po Box 2014
Ivanhoe East Vic 3079
Australia

First published in Australia 2024


National Library of Australia Cataloguing in Publication entry

 A catalogue record for this book is available from the National Library of Australia

ISBN: 978-1-7635578-0-2 (paperback)
ISBN: 978-1-7635578-1-9 (hardcover)
ISBN: 978-1-7635578-2-6 (epub)

Layout and design by Sophie White Design

Printed by IngramSpark

# A Single Woman's Sassy Guide

## YOGA, READING, SISTERS, AND WINE

Elizabeth Jane Danin

# Contents

# Introduction

*Women, whether subtly or vociferously, have always been a tremendous power in the destiny of the world.*

ELEANOR ROOSEVELT

This declaration is not just an observation but a testament to the indomitable spirit that resides within every woman. It's a reminder that throughout history, in the shadows and in the spotlight, women have been the architects of change, the bearers of wisdom, and the unsung heroes of progress.

In a world that often feels like it's spinning too fast, where the roles and expectations placed upon us can feel as heavy as they are endless, there exists a sanctuary. It's not a place, but a recipe for balance, joy, and health—a blend of practices and pleasures that can transform the mundane into the magical. Let this book be your guide in concocting a powerful potion, specifically tailored for the single woman navigating the complexities of modern life. This book is crafted not just as a guide, but as a companion. It whispers the ancient wisdom of yoga, a practice that stretches and strengthens not just the body, but the soul. Yoga serves as our foundation, a reminder that in the midst of chaos, there is a pose, a breath, a moment of stillness that can bring us back to our center.

Then, there's reading—a voyage into the depths of other worlds, other lives, and other perspectives. Books are mirrors and windows; they reflect our own experiences and offer views into lives we might never lead. This book celebrates reading as a form of self-care, an escape, and a tool for growth, proposing a diverse library that entertains, enlightens, and empowers. Sisters, be they by blood or bond, are the heartbeat of this elixir. They are the ones who laugh and cry with us, who offer wine when the world offers worries. This section of the book delves into the art of nurturing these relationships, recognizing the power of sisterhood in healing, supporting, and elevating one another. It's about creating and sustaining connections that feed the soul and foster resilience against life's trials.

And, of course, wine—the liquid ruby that has been a symbol of transformation and celebration for centuries. Whether enjoying a quiet glass alone after a long day or sharing a bottle with friends, wine can be a delightful complement to a well-rounded life. This book explores the ritual of wine tasting and appreciation, weaving it into the fabric of self-care and social bonding, all while promoting moderation and mindfulness.

*A Single Woman's Sassy Guide* is more than a book; it's a movement toward embracing solitude not as a sign of lacking, but as an opportunity for growth and self-discovery. It's a call to live deliberately and joyously, finding health and happiness in the simple pleasures of life. Through yoga, reading, sisters, and wine, this guide offers tools and inspiration for the single woman to craft a life of balance, depth, and connection. Join us on this journey to sip, stretch, read, and bond your way to a more vibrant and healthy life.

In wrapping up, there's the tale of the single woman who decided to bring her own cheer squad everywhere. Why? Because life, with its ups and downs, could use a bit more applause. Picture this: She finishes a presentation at work—cheers erupt from her purse. She makes her morning coffee—standing ovation from the kitchen counter. And when she finally figures out her taxes, it's like she's won an Oscar, with confetti dropping from the ceiling. So, to all the remarkable single women: may your days be filled with self-made fanfare, because sometimes, the most deserving of applause is the one you give yourself. After all, who says you can't be your own biggest cheerleader in the comedy show of life?

# CHAPTER 1

# The Art of Balancing on One Leg

Standing on one leg isn't just a demonstration of physical skill or a fun trick for social gatherings; it symbolizes the intricate challenge of finding balance amidst the tumult of singlehood. The yoga mat turns into a sanctuary, a place where the turmoil of unread messages and societal pressures to 'find someone' dissipate with every focused inhalation in downward dog position. Indeed, wine seems to acquire a richer taste after engaging in a warrior pose, likely because each gulp serves as a tribute to both your bodily and emotional adaptability. Furthermore, when faced with the inevitable flood of unasked-for opinions at family events, adeptness in breathing exercises becomes an invaluable ally, rendering inquiries about your marital status to nothing more than background noise.

## The Yoga Mat as Your Personal Island

Yoga offers a myriad of benefits tailored to the unique physiological and emotional landscapes of single women, fostering a sense of balance and well-being through various life stages. Here's a concise overview:

- **Hormonal Balance:** Regular practice helps mitigate symptoms related to menstrual cycles, pregnancy, and menopause, such as mood swings, bloating, and hot flashes.

- **Pain Relief:** Specific poses can alleviate menstrual cramps by enhancing circulation to the abdominal region, while the meditative aspect of yoga soothes the mind.

- **Improved Physical Health:** Increases in flexibility, balance, and strength are notable benefits, with many feeling more robust after just one session.

- **Cardio-Metabolic Health:** Yoga aids in improving blood circulation and reducing heart disease risks, offering support to those undergoing cancer treatments or dealing with Alzheimer's.

- **Mental Wellness:** By promoting inner reflection and focusing on the breath, yoga significantly reduces anxiety and depression, enhancing mental clarity and emotional balance.

- **Sleep Quality:** Incorporating yoga into nighttime routines can lead to more restful sleep, with specific poses designed to prepare the body and mind for rest.

- **Stress Management:** The practice pulls focus away from daily stressors, grounding individuals in the present and improving overall well-being through mindfulness and relaxation techniques.

Yoga, with its combination of physical postures, mental relaxation, and breath work, stands as a powerful tool for single women to navigate the complexities of life with enhanced physical and emotional resilience.

## Discovering Inner Peace in Downward Dog

Downward Facing Dog, or *Adho Mukha Svanasana*, is more than just a physical stretch; it's a gateway to inner peace for single women navigating the complexities of modern life. This pose, mimicking the natural stretching of a dog, offers a unique blend of physical benefits and mental tranquility that can be particularly empowering.

Firstly, the physical aspect of the pose stretches the hamstrings and calves, areas where many of us hold tension and stress. For single women, who often juggle numerous responsibilities and face societal pressures, releasing this physical tension is the first step toward achieving mental relaxation. The elongation of the spine and the strengthening of the shoulders in this pose also contribute to a feeling of bodily release and openness, which can be especially liberating.

As an inversion, Downward Facing Dog shifts your perspective, literally turning the world upside down. This physical change of view can symbolize a shift in mental outlook, encouraging openness to new perspectives and possibilities. It's a reminder that sometimes looking at things from a different angle can lead to deeper insights and solutions. Moreover, the pose demands focus and breathing, key components of mindfulness, which draws your attention away from the whirlwind of thoughts and concerns that may clutter your mind. This moment of connection between body and breath serves as a powerful tool for centering and grounding oneself, fostering a sense of present-moment awareness that is essential for inner peace.

In practicing Downward Facing Dog, single women engage in a deliberate act of self-care and self-attention. It's a moment to prioritize one's well-being, setting aside external pressures and expectations. The strength and stability required to maintain the pose reflect the inner strength and resilience that single women possess, reminding them of their capacity to support and uplift themselves. Through regular practice, Downward Facing Dog becomes more than a physical exercise; it transforms into a meditative experience that nurtures the mind, body, and spirit. It offers a sanctuary of calm and stability amidst the chaos of daily life, a place where single women can return to themselves, find their center, and cultivate a deep sense of inner peace.

## Linking Relaxation and Indulgence

For single women seeking to enhance their well-being, indulging in a daily glass of wine isn't just about savoring the flavor; it's a journey toward vitality and serenity. Here's why it's worth raising a toast to your health (Breyer, 2022):

- **Antioxidant Oasis:** Dive into a world of antioxidants found abundantly in wine, especially red varieties. These powerful compounds, like polyphenols and resveratrol, act as shields for your cells, warding off threats of diseases like cancer and heart issues.

- **Heartfelt Benefits:** Pour yourself a glass of heart health with wine's ability to curb plaque buildup in arteries, elevate "good" HDL cholesterol levels, and potentially lower the risk of heart attacks, strokes, and diabetes. It's like a sip of love for your cardiovascular system.

- **Gut-Healthy Goodness:** Explore the diverse ecosystem of bacteria thriving in the guts of red wine enthusiasts. This bustling community not only promotes gut health but may also ward off pesky digestive woes like gallstones, keeping your tummy happy and thriving.

- **Cheers to Mental Wellness:** Delve into the realm of resveratrol, a red wine treasure known for its potential to fend off feelings of anxiety and depression by taming stress-related enzymes in the brain. Plus, the simple act of unwinding with a glass of wine can whisk you away from life's stresses, offering a moment of tranquility in a bustling world.

In essence, wine isn't just a beverage; it's a catalyst for a vibrant and balanced life for single women. So, pour yourself a glass, raise it high, and toast to your health, happiness, and the journey ahead.

## Why Wine Tastes Better After Warrior Pose

The experience of savoring a glass of wine after practicing Warrior Pose (*Virabhadrasana I*) goes beyond mere physical refreshment; it is an embodiment of the harmony between relaxation and indulgence, a ritual that intertwines the pleasures of the body and the serenity of the spirit. This phenomenon, where wine tastes better post-yoga, particularly after engaging in the strength and focus of Warrior Pose, can be attributed to several interconnected factors that enhance the sensory experience.

Firstly, Warrior Pose, a foundational element in yoga practice, engages the body in a powerful stance, grounding the practitioner firmly to the earth while reaching upwards and outwards, embodying the strength and fearlessness of the mythical warrior *Virabhadra*.

This pose is not just about physical alignment; it's a practice in concentration and breath control, demanding mental presence and discipline. The exertion of maintaining the pose, coupled with deep, mindful breathing, catalyzes a holistic engagement of the body and mind, priming the senses for heightened awareness.

Upon transitioning from such an immersive state of focus and strength to the act of wine tasting, the body is in a heightened state of relaxation. The physical exertion and subsequent release into relaxation trigger the release of endorphins, enhancing mood and creating a sense of well-being. This physiological shift not only relaxes the body but also opens the mind to deeper sensory experiences. Wine, with its complex layers of aroma, taste, and texture, is thus experienced more intensely and enjoyably after the heightened sensory awareness brought on by yoga practice.

Moreover, the deliberate, mindful breathing practiced in Warrior Pose enhances one's olfactory senses, crucial for appreciating the nuanced flavors of wine. The act of focusing on the breath helps to slow down and deepen the wine-tasting experience, encouraging a more thoughtful and engaged approach to savoring each sip.

The ritual of enjoying wine after yoga, especially after the intensity and focus of Warrior Pose, embodies a celebration of balance—between strength and relaxation, discipline and indulgence. It symbolizes a rewarding moment of pause, a conscious choice to indulge in the pleasures of life with gratitude and presence, deeply rooted in the moment. This practice acknowledges that indulgence, when approached with mindfulness and balance, can be an integral part of a well-rounded life, enhancing the appreciation of simple pleasures through a lens of relaxation and well-being.

In essence, the enhanced taste of wine after Warrior Pose is not just about the physical benefits of yoga but about how the practice enriches the experience of indulgence, making it a mindful, deeply satisfying encounter with the senses, grounded in the present moment.

# Breathing Techniques for Dodging Unwanted Advice

Picture this: You're at a family gathering, surrounded by well-meaning relatives who just can't resist asking about your love life. The pressure mounts as questions about when you'll settle down and find a partner start pouring in. It's enough to make anyone feel flustered and overwhelmed. But amidst the chaos, there's a secret weapon at your disposal: mindful breathing.

Mindful breathing isn't just a trendy wellness trend; it's a superhero cape you can wear anytime, anywhere. Imagine it as your trusty sidekick, ready to swoop in and save the day when unwanted advice comes knocking. With just a few intentional breaths, you can transform tense moments into opportunities for calm and clarity.

Here's how it works: By tuning into the rhythm of your breath, you anchor yourself in the present moment, creating a buffer against the onslaught of intrusive questions. As you inhale deeply and exhale slowly, you create space within yourself to respond thoughtfully rather than react impulsively. It's like hitting the pause button on stress and dialing up your inner strength. And the best part? Mindful breathing is a portable power-up that fits right in your pocket. There are no fancy gadgets required—just you and your breath, working in perfect harmony to shield you from unwanted advice and keep your cool intact.

So, the next time Aunt Mildred starts prying into your love life, take a deep breath and let mindfulness be your guide. With each inhale and exhale, you'll find yourself standing taller, speaking with confidence, and gracefully sidestepping those well-meaning but oh-so-irksome questions. Mindful breathing isn't just a technique; it's your secret weapon for dodging unwanted advice like a boss.

# Using Pranayama to Maintain Sanity in Social Gatherings

Let's delve into the art of breathwork, exploring its profound impact on our well-being. Beyond merely sustaining life, our breath serves as a gateway to deeper realms of consciousness. What we commonly perceive as breath is but the tangible manifestation of a more subtle force known as Prana, or vital energy. Pranayama, the practice of harnessing this energy through breath manipulation, holds a central place in yoga philosophy, offering a pathway to inner transformation.

Pranayama is indispensable for anyone embarking on an inner journey, as it facilitates the regulation of life-sustaining processes within the body. Through various techniques, practitioners gain control over their breath, thereby influencing the flow of Prana throughout their being. This vital energy, akin to the life force coursing through the universe, permeates every aspect of our existence, sustaining our physical and mental well-being.

In the practice of Pranayama, the intricate dance of respiration within the lungs is consciously regulated, allowing individuals to direct and channel their Prana with intention. Just as our circulatory system distributes blood, so too does Prana flow through a network of energy pathways known as *Nadis*, vitalizing every cell and organ. Yet, modern lifestyles often disrupt this flow, leading to sluggishness and diminished vitality. Pranayama acts as a catalyst for restoring the natural rhythm of Prana, infusing the body with dynamism and vigor.

Ancient sages likened those unaware of their Prana to birds tethered to a post, unable to soar freely. Similarly, a restless mind finds solace and equilibrium in the harmonious flow of Prana. Mastery over Prana grants mastery over the mind itself, ushering in a state of profound clarity and serenity.

However, the practice of Pranayama demands caution and guidance, as its effects on the subtle energies of the body are potent and immediate. Adequate preparation, both physically and mentally, is essential before embarking on this transformative journey.

Some traditions advocate for rigorous physical conditioning and steadfastness in yogic postures before commencing Pranayama, ensuring readiness for the profound shifts it engenders.

For those dedicated to the path of Pranayama, steadfastness and diligence yield remarkable progress in a relatively short span of time. Yet, half-hearted efforts yield scant rewards. Pranayama is a potent tool for self-discovery and inner mastery, but only for those willing to approach it with reverence, commitment, and perseverance.

Before delving into the practice of Pranayama, it's crucial to understand its fundamental components. Pranayama encompasses three primary actions: inhalation (*puraka*), exhalation (*rechaka*), and the vital breath retention (*kumbhaka*). Breath retention, in particular, holds immense significance in Pranayama. When executed methodically, breath retention enhances vitality, vigor, and mental acuity. It's believed that for every minute we retain the breath, our lifespan extends by one minute.

To begin your Pranayama practice, aim for one or two sessions per day initially, gradually increasing to four sessions over time. Space out your practices evenly throughout the day, ideally incorporating a session during *Brahma muhurta*, the auspicious period before sunrise. It's essential to practice Pranayama on an empty stomach for optimal results.

Now, if you find yourself in need of grounding and sanity during social gatherings, consider practicing *Kapalbhati Pranayama*. This technique, translating to "skull shining breath," cleanses the frontal brain and invigorates the mind. To practice *Kapalbhati Pranayama*:

1.  Sit comfortably with a straight spine and relaxed shoulders.

2.  Exhale forcefully through both nostrils, contracting the abdominal muscles.

3.  Allow the inhalation to occur naturally, without exerting effort.

4.  Complete ten rapid exhalations followed by a brief pause to allow the breath to return to normal.

5.  Repeat this cycle for up to five rounds.

*Kapalbhati Pranayama* is an ideal starting point for beginners, offering benefits such as improved respiratory and circulatory functions. With consistent practice and proper guidance, you'll gradually deepen your understanding of Pranayama and harness its transformative potential for enhanced well-being.

As you embark on your yoga journey, envision your yoga mat as your personal island—a sanctuary where you find solace and inner peace. From the tranquility of Downward Dog to the empowering strength of Warrior Pose, embrace the connection between relaxation and indulgence. Notice how a sip of wine tastes even sweeter after the challenge of a yoga session and use mindful breathing as your secret weapon to navigate social gatherings with grace. Let Pranayama be your steadfast ally, guiding you through life's twists and turns with resilience and serenity. Together, these practices weave a tapestry of self-discovery and empowerment, inviting you to embrace the beauty of balance and find harmony within yourself and the world around you.

After mastering the Downward Dog, savoring wine post-Warrior Pose, and breathing through unsolicited life advice, it's clear we're not just finding inner peace—we're basically becoming zen sommeliers of life's chaotic social gatherings. Remember, if you can't find your zen in the noise, there's always the pose of 'Sipping Merlot in Solitude'. Cheers to navigating the party of life, one breath (and sip) at a time!

# CHAPTER 2

# Building Your Library Like Your Wine Cellar

Embark on a journey where your bookshelf becomes as curated as a fine wine cellar, blending the art of literature with the craft of winemaking. Envision novels as the Merlot of your collection—smooth, enveloping, perfect for unwinding. Non-fiction stands as the bold Cabernet Sauvignon, challenging your palate and mind alike. In the world where the unpredictability of life mirrors a mystery novel, the wisdom within these pages comforts like your favorite vintage. Bridging book clubs and wine clubs is more than indulgence; it's a sophisticated dance of tastes and texts, where declaring a "book budget" can cleverly mask your vinous adventures. Here, each selection, be it page or pour, is an ode to the rich tapestry of experiences awaiting discovery.

## Novels, Non-Fiction, and Merlot: Pairing Books With the Perfect Glass

Why limit the joy of pairing to just food and wine when you can extend it to your literary adventures as well? Embark on a whimsical journey through the pages of literature and the vineyards of wine, where each sip and sentence intertwine to create a symphony of taste and tale. Picture yourself in a cozy corner, surrounded by the gentle hum of the seasons, a glass of your favorite vintage in hand, and a book brimming with adventure awaiting your eager eyes. But this is no ordinary reading session; this is a carefully curated experience where the pairing of wine and words becomes an art form, a delightful dance of flavor and fantasy.

Let us begin this enchanting escapade by considering the time of year, both in the real world and within the pages of your chosen book. Are you basking in the warmth of summer's embrace, with the sun-kissed breeze whispering through open windows? Or are you nestled by the fireplace, cocooned in the cozy blanket of winter's chill? The season sets the stage for your literary and vinous adventure, guiding your selection toward wine that mirrors the spirit of the moment—crisp and refreshing whites for summer's languid days, or rich, velvety reds to warm your soul during winter's embrace.

But the magic doesn't stop there. Take a moment to consider the setting of your story—whether it's the sun-drenched vineyards of Italy or the bustling streets of New York City. Let the narrative's locale be your guide as you select a bottle of wine that hails from the same region, allowing the flavors of the landscape to intertwine with the essence of the story. As you sip on a glass of Chianti while immersed in the Tuscan countryside of a beloved novel, you'll find yourself transported to a world where every sip is infused with the aroma of olive groves and rolling hills.

Now, let's add a dash of humor and a sprinkle of creativity to this literary libation. Consider the genre and tone of your book—whether it's a swashbuckling adventure or a cozy mystery—and let your wine selection reflect the mood of the narrative. Are you exploring the treacherous intrigues of a medieval epic like *Game of Thrones*? Why not indulge in a glass of mulled wine, infused with spices and warmth, to evoke the rugged landscapes of Westeros? Or perhaps you're delving into the pages of a lighthearted romance, where the air is sweet with the promise of love and laughter. In that case, reach for a delicate rosé, its blush hues echoing the rosy glow of budding romance.

But wait, there's more! Let's not forget to tailor your wine selection to match the energy of your reading environment. Are you stealing moments of solitude amidst the chaos of family life, with children's laughter providing a soundtrack to your literary adventures? Or do you find solace in the quiet hours of the night, with only the soft glow of a lamp to illuminate the pages before you? Match your wine choices to the tempo of your surroundings—whether it's a lively, effervescent pour to keep pace with the laughter of children or a deep, contemplative vintage to savor in the stillness of the night.

And finally, let us raise a glass to the joy of literary and vinous exploration, where every sip and page holds the promise of adventure and discovery. In this delightful confluence of taste and tale, where wine and words dance in harmony, there are no rules—only endless possibilities waiting to be savored. So, pour yourself a glass, settle into your favorite reading spot, and let the magic of wine and words whisk you away on an unforgettable journey. Cheers to the whimsy of wine and words, where every combination is a delightful adventure waiting to be savored!

## Book Clubs vs. Wine Clubs: Why You Need Both, or Just an Excuse for More Wine

Why bother with clubs when you can indulge in solitary reading and drinking sessions, you might wonder? Let's delve into the world of book clubs first. One of the foremost advantages of joining a book club, especially for those seeking to rekindle their love for reading, lies in its accountability factor. By becoming a member, you commit to devouring the book of the month (or week) alongside fellow enthusiasts. The fear of letting down your peers serves as a powerful motivator to dive into the pages, ensuring you stay on track with your reading goals. Additionally, participation in book club discussions fosters a deeper engagement with the material. If you're accustomed to racing through books, the prospect of dissecting them with others may encourage you to savor each word, leading to a more profound understanding and appreciation of the text. Moreover, the diverse backgrounds and perspectives of fellow club members enrich discussions, offering fresh insights and opening your mind to viewpoints you may not have considered otherwise.

However, it's essential to navigate these diverse perspectives with grace and respect, as disagreements can arise. Yet, these potential conflicts are outweighed by the opportunity to forge new friendships. Joining a book club not only provides an avenue for intellectual discourse but also serves as a social platform to connect with like-minded individuals who share your passion for literature.

Now, let's uncork the benefits of wine clubs. Feeling overwhelmed by the plethora of wine options at your disposal is a sentiment shared by many oenophiles. Enter the wine club—an oasis of guidance in this vast sea of vintages. Through tailored selections curated to suit your palate preferences, wine clubs eliminate the guesswork, ensuring you receive bottles that resonate with your taste buds. No more aimless wandering through aisles; your personalized wine journey is delivered straight to your doorstep.

Beyond convenience, wine clubs wield considerable purchasing power, translating into savings for members. Exclusive discounts, special promotions, and loyalty rewards sweeten the deal, offering not only exceptional wines but also affordability. But the perks don't end there. Many clubs offer access to exclusive events, such as wine tastings and sessions with expert sommeliers, transforming wine appreciation into a holistic learning experience. In essence, joining a wine club isn't merely about enjoying wine—it's about expanding your knowledge, refining your palate, and embarking on a journey of vinous discovery.

Indulge in the ultimate blend of brainpower and liquid courage with dual club membership! Join both the captivating realms of book and wine clubs, where laughter, gossip, and perhaps a touch too much vino await.

Imagine this: you've just finished a particularly riveting chapter of your book club's latest selection, and you're feeling inspired to channel your inner Elizabeth Bennet. But wait—what's that? Your wine club delivery has just arrived, and it's filled to the brim with tantalizing bottles just waiting to be uncorked. Suddenly, your cozy night in with Mr. Darcy takes a turn for the tipsy as you find yourself indulging in a solo dance party to the smooth tunes of Frank Sinatra, fueled by a glass (or two) of that delicious sauvignon blanc you've been eyeing all week.

But the real fun begins when your sisters come over for a gossip session. With your book club selections spread out on the coffee table and a selection of fine wines at the ready, you dive into juicy discussions about everything from the latest celebrity scandals to the romantic escapades of your favorite literary heroes. And as the night wears on and the wine flows freely, the stories become even more outrageous, the laughter even louder, and the bonds of sisterhood even stronger.

Of course, no book and wine club gathering would be complete without a few amusing mishaps along the way. Who can forget the time Sarah accidentally spilled red wine on her brand-new white carpet during a heated debate about the ending of *Gone Girl*? Or the time Emily tried to open a bottle of champagne with a kitchen knife and ended up sending the cork flying across the room, narrowly missing poor Bella's head?

But despite the occasional spills and thrills, one thing is for sure: joining both a book club and a wine club is the ultimate recipe for singlehood success. So, to all the single ladies out there, why waste your time swiping through endless profiles when you could be indulging in brainy banter and liquid courage with your fellow bookworms and wine enthusiasts? Cheers to embracing the single life with style, sass, and plenty of literary libations!

## "I'm on a Book Budget": The Fine Art of Library Loans and Bargain Bins

Ah, the enchanting realm of libraries—a treasure trove of literary delights beckoning you to embark on whimsical adventures, even when your purse strings are feeling a bit tight. Close your eyes and cast your mind back to the days of your youth, when stepping into the library was akin to entering a magical kingdom, brimming with untold stories and undiscovered wonders. That sense of anticipation and excitement? It's still there, waiting to be rediscovered in the nooks and crannies of your local library.

Now, let's talk about deadlines. Yes, those seemingly pesky due dates can actually work wonders for your reading habits. Picture this: you've borrowed a book from the library, and you know you have a limited time to return it. Suddenly, that book becomes a thrilling race against the clock—a literary adventure waiting to unfold. No more letting books languish on your shelf, gathering dust like forgotten relics of bygone days. With a deadline looming, you'll be motivated to dive into the pages and savor every word.

But hold onto your bookmarks, because there's more! Librarians aren't just keepers of books; they're like magical beings with the power to unlock new worlds and unearth hidden treasures. Need a recommendation for your next literary escapade? Simply summon a librarian, and they'll sprinkle their fairy dust of wisdom and guide you to the perfect read. Whether you're craving a spine-tingling thriller or a heartwarming romance, they've got you covered.

And let's dispel a myth right now: being on a budget doesn't mean you have to skimp on your reading adventures. Oh no, my dear book lover, the library is here to save the day! With shelves stacked high with a cornucopia of books just waiting to be borrowed, you can indulge your literary cravings without spending a single penny. It's like having your own personal bookstore, minus the hefty price tags.

But wait, there's more! Libraries aren't just about borrowing books; they're vibrant community hubs bursting with activity. From lively storytimes that transport you to faraway lands to summer reading programs that ignite your imagination, there's never a dull moment at the library. And let's not forget about the book clubs, used book sales, and other events that bring bookworms together in a delightful celebration of all things literary.

So, dear budget-savvy book lover, why limit yourself when the library offers so much more? Dive headfirst into a world of endless literary possibilities, explore new genres, and connect with fellow bookworms—all without breaking the bank. The library awaits, ready to fuel your literary adventures with its boundless treasures.

In the world of literature, you can also opt to buy bargain books, unlocking a treasure trove of affordable reading delights. Who says you have to break the bank to indulge your literary cravings? Why drop a hefty $30 on a brand-new hardcover that'll end up gathering dust on your shelf like a glorified paperweight? Fear not, savvy readers, for there's a treasure trove of bargain books waiting to be discovered!

Picture this: you stroll into a quaint used book store or stumble upon a yard sale, and there, nestled among the shelves, you find a gem of a novel for just a dollar. Yes, you read that right—books for a dollar! These second-hand treasures may not be in pristine condition, but who cares when you're getting a steal of a deal? But wait, there's more! If you're feeling bold, why not try your hand at a little friendly bartering? Negotiate with the owners and see if you can snag an even better bargain, especially if you're buying multiple books. After all, every dollar saved is a dollar earned, right?

And let's not forget about supporting your local community. Instead of lining the pockets of big-box retailers, opt to buy from small, second-hand stores. Not only do you score great deals, but you also get to connect with local bookstore owners and fellow bookworms. Who knows, you might even stumble upon author Q&As or weekly book clubs, opening the door to a whole new world of literary adventures. But perhaps the best part of buying used books is the opportunity to give back. By supporting stores that promote recycling and reusing, you affirm the value of second-hand products and help keep these community hubs thriving. And when you're ready to part ways with your beloved books, consider donating them to spread the joy of reading to others.

As you embark on the delightful journey of pairing books with the perfect glass, don't forget the essential companions: book clubs and wine clubs. Whether you're exploring the depths of a novel, uncovering truths in non-fiction, or indulging in the smooth complexity of Merlot, these clubs offer the ultimate blend of literary and libational pleasures. So, embrace the "book budget" with library loans and bargain bins, but never underestimate the joy of sharing stories over a glass of wine. After all, as they say, "I'm on a Book Budget" sounds much more responsible than "I spent all my money on wine...again." Cheers to the perfect pairing!

# CHAPTER 3

# Sisterhood: The Other Soulmates

Who says soulmates have to come in the form of a swoon-worthy romantic partner? I'm a proud member of the sisterhood, where the bond is thicker than the chunkiest pint of chocolate fudge ice cream. These are the ladies who know the difference between "fine" and "grab the wine", who show up with a bottle and a shoulder to cry on faster than you can say "bad day". Our group chats are like the modern-day equivalent of a secret society, where we share everything from juicy gossip to life-altering advice, all wrapped up in a package of unabashed support.

In a world where distances can stretch longer than the line at a trendy brunch spot, my sisterhood thrives on creativity. We've mastered the art of virtual happy hours via Skype, perfected the ancient ritual of sending heartfelt letters via snail mail, and we're not afraid to pop up unannounced for surprise visits that leave us laughing until our sides ache. Because, let's face it, home isn't just a place with four walls and a roof—it's a feeling you get when you're surrounded by the women who truly get you.

# Choosing Your Family: Why Friends Are the Sisters Fate Forgot to Give You

Friendship sisterhood is like stumbling upon the sisters fate forgot to include in your family tree. It's a bond so deep, it feels like they've been a part of your life since the beginning of time. Beyond the casual hangouts and juicy gossip sessions, it's about an unshakeable love, trust, understanding, and unwavering support through life's highs and lows, no matter what curveballs fate throws your way. These are the sisters you choose, the ones who stand by you through thick and thin, making the journey of life a little less lonely and a lot more joyful.

Forget the plot of a sappy romance novel—this is the real deal, folks! Friendship turned into sisterhood is like upgrading from a cozy one-bedroom apartment to a sprawling mansion complete with a pool and a personal chef. It's the kind of bond that transcends mere friendship and dives headfirst into the realm of sisterhood, where trust, loyalty, support, and understanding reign supreme.

Picture this: You and your gal pal, navigating life's rollercoaster together, armed with inside jokes, shared secrets, and a stash of emergency chocolate for those inevitable meltdown moments. This isn't just any old friendship; it's a full-blown sisterhood, where you're each other's ride-or-die, confidante, and partner-in-crime all rolled into one fabulous package. So, throw away the rulebook on conventional friendships, because when it comes to sisterhood, there are no limits. It's like finding your soulmate, but instead of swiping right, you just clicked over shared interests and a mutual love for bottomless brunches.

The journey from friendship to sisterhood is a nuanced one, requiring dedication, love, and a sprinkle of spontaneity. Here's a roadmap to transform your friendship into a bond that rivals even the strongest of sisterhoods:

- **Presence is Paramount:** Show up for each other during life's pivotal moments—birthdays, weddings, or those monumental promotions. Celebrate each other's victories as if they were your own, for in sisterhood, every triumph is shared.

· **Listen with Intent:** Deep connections are forged through attentive listening. Show compassion by truly understanding your friend's perspective, while also maintaining healthy boundaries.

· **Gratitude is Key:** Never underestimate the power of a simple "thank you." Expressing gratitude fosters a deeper emotional connection, nurturing your relationship for years to come.

· **Embrace Honest Communication:** Trust is the cornerstone of sisterhood, and honesty is its building block. Speak your truth openly, without fear of judgment, and create a safe space where your friend feels free to do the same.

· **Create Lasting Memories:** Shared experiences are the glue that binds sisterhoods together. From spontaneous road trips to volunteering together, cherish these moments as the foundation of your bond.

· **Support, Support, Support:** As sisters, your role is to uplift and empower each other. Recognize and celebrate each other's unique strengths, and stand firm as a pillar of support through life's inevitable storms.

· **Unwavering Advocacy:** True sisters stand side by side in the face of adversity. Whether it's navigating familial disagreements or confronting workplace challenges, be each other's fiercest advocate.

When two friends embody these principles, they morph into sisters—royalty amidst the branches of the family tree! Come what may, life's tumultuous tides won't wrench them asunder but bind them closer. It's a bond surpassing the ordinary, one capable of weathering the ages.

In conclusion, cultivating sisterhood from friendship necessitates dedication, affection, reliance, endeavor, and mutual admiration. While instantaneous transformation eludes us, investing in one another is an endeavor of immeasurable value. For when the stars align, this bond transcends time, enduring eternally. So, let's raise our glasses to the power of sisterhood—a force to reckon with, everlasting and unwavering. Cheers to forever friendships!

## Group Chats, Gossip, and Guidance: Navigating Life's Ups and Downs With a Support Squad

Navigating the intricate landscape of singlehood often feels akin to straddling a thrilling yet unpredictable rollercoaster. The highs come with an intoxicating sense of freedom and the liberty to chart one's own course, untethered by the obligations or expectations of a partner. On the flip side, the lows can plunge you into moments of solitude, sparking introspective questions about one's place and purpose within the vast tapestry of human connection.

Single life is frequently characterized as a transient phase, a sort of liminal space filled with anticipation for what or who comes next. Society frames it as a period of waiting—a pause in the narrative, eagerly anticipating the arrival of a soulmate, the commencement of family life, or some other relationship milestone. Yet, this perspective overlooks the richness and vitality of the single experience as a standalone chapter, brimming with potential for self-exploration and personal evolution.

Amidst this journey, the sisterhood of friends emerges as an invaluable treasure, transforming singlehood from a solo voyage into a shared adventure. This bond, forged not by blood but by mutual respect, empathy, and unwavering support, serves as a cornerstone for both personal and communal growth. It's in this space that being single transcends societal expectations, morphing into a powerful phase of transformation and empowerment.

The single phase offers a fertile ground for diving into the depths of self-discovery. It's an uninterrupted stretch of time allowing for introspection, self-care, and an unapologetic pursuit of personal aspirations. This period empowers individuals to explore the world, indulge in new hobbies, and expand social horizons without the need to align with a partner's desires or life plan. The freedom to embark on spontaneous adventures, cultivate new skills, or simply revel in the joy of one's own company can be profoundly liberating.

Yet, it's the presence of "sisters" in this journey that truly enriches the experience. These are the friends who morph into family, offering a scaffolding of support through the solitary stretches and celebratory moments alike. They are the ones who light up the path through the darker patches, offering solace, encouragement, and a sense of belonging. In moments of doubt or loneliness, reaching out to this chosen family can provide a lifeline, a reminder that solitude does not equate to isolation.

Building a robust network of support is essential, serving a dual purpose. In times of turmoil or uncertainty, this sisterhood offers a comforting embrace, a safe space to unravel and seek guidance. Conversely, in moments of triumph and joy, these are the cheerleaders amplifying your successes, magnifying the sweetness of every achievement. This sisterly bond underscores the notion that one's value and fulfillment need not be tethered to romantic conquests but can flourish in the camaraderie and solidarity shared among friends.

Navigating singlehood, therefore, should not be misconstrued as a journey of solitude but rather as an opportunity to weave a rich tapestry of relationships that celebrate individuality and mutual upliftment. The sisterhood that accompanies this phase acts as a testament to the enduring strength and beauty of platonic love, underscoring the fact that being single is a chapter replete with its own unique joys, challenges, and opportunities for growth.

It is within the laughter, shared stories, and collective wisdom of these sisterly bonds that the true essence of singlehood is revealed—not as a period of lacking but as a vibrant stage of life overflowing with potential. These relationships provide a backdrop against which the adventures of single life unfold, enriching each experience and providing a sense of continuity and belonging.

In embracing the single journey with your sisters by your side, every moment becomes an occasion for growth, discovery, and joy. The group chats buzz with activity, brimming with gossip, advice, and unwavering support. Each interaction, each shared experience, serves to deepen the bonds of this chosen family, reinforcing the notion that while the journey may be embarked upon alone, the path is lined with the hearts and souls of those we choose to call our sisters.

Thus, the narrative of singlehood is transformed. It becomes a celebration of autonomy, a testament to the strength found in sisterhood, and a reminder that life's fullest expression often lies beyond the conventional markers of relationship status. In this light, singlehood is not a waiting room but a vibrant arena for growth, with sisterhood at its heart, offering a shared journey through the ups and downs, always reminding us that even in our solitary moments, we are never truly alone.

## Sisterhood Across Time Zones: Keeping Connections Strong With Skype, Snail Mail, and Spontaneous Visits

In an era where digital connectivity has bridged the vast expanses separating us, nurturing long-distance sisterhoods has become more achievable and rewarding than ever before. Despite the physical miles that may lie between you and your sisters-at-heart, a plethora of tools and tactics are at your disposal to ensure that the emotional distance is kept to a minimum. Indeed, maintaining these precious bonds requires effort and commitment from all parties involved, but the payoff—a lifelong friendship that withstands the tests of time and distance—is immeasurably worth it. From engaging in virtual coffee catch-ups to the joy of receiving an unexpected care package, let's explore how you can fortify your connections with your long-distance besties, ensuring that your sisterly bond remains as strong and vibrant as ever.

· Embrace the Power of Photography and Written Words: Regularly exchange photos and updates about your lives. A simple meme that captures an inside joke or a heartfelt letter can bridge the gap between you, making the physical distance seem trivial.

· Establish and Honor Routines: Consistency is key. Set aside time for monthly virtual get-togethers—be it over coffee or cocktails. Regular check-ins, even if just for a quick chat over the weekend, can keep the sense of closeness alive.

· Share Experiences: Simultaneously watching a movie or diving into the same book can give you both a common ground for discussions, significantly shrinking the emotional distance between you.

· Uphold Core Values: Honesty, reliability, and appreciation are the pillars of any strong relationship. These values gain even more significance in a long-distance sisterhood, ensuring that trust and mutual respect continue to flourish.

· Make Time for Each Other: Whether through scheduled meetings or spontaneous calls, seeing each other's expressions via video chat can significantly enhance the quality of your interactions, making every conversation more meaningful.

· Communicate With Transparency and Understanding: In today's always-on culture, it's vital to set clear expectations about communication preferences. Transparency about your availability and response times can prevent misunderstandings and foster a healthy, stress-free relationship.

By incorporating these strategies into your long-distance friendships, you not only overcome the challenge of separation but also reinforce the foundation of your relationship, ensuring that it remains robust regardless of the miles that separate you. Whether through the simplicity of sharing a meme that sparks joy, the anticipation of a monthly virtual meeting, or the shared experience of a book that touched both your hearts, these moments of connection serve to remind you that true sisterhood knows no boundaries.

The journey of maintaining a long-distance sisterhood is filled with both challenges and rewards. It's about finding joy in the small gestures, the comfort in shared silence over a video call, and the excitement in planning your next reunion. It's a testament to the fact that, even in a world where physical presence is often missed, the bonds of friendship and sisterhood can thrive, nurtured by love, effort, and the myriad tools technology offers us.

In essence, these friendships become a beacon of unwavering support, laughter, and companionship, shining brightly across the miles. They remind us that distance is but a minor obstacle when it comes to the profound connections of the heart. So, embrace these tips, pour love and effort into your long-distance sisterhoods, and watch as these bonds grow even stronger, proving that true friendship isn't about being inseparable—it's about being separated and nothing changes.

Navigating through the saga of selecting our own squad and knitting tight-knit connections across continents, we've uncovered that friends are indeed the sisters destiny forgot to drop off at our doorstep. Armed with memes, midnight confessions, and the magical ability to turn every group chat into an epic saga of laughter and support, this chosen family proves that you don't need shared DNA to have someone's back or to borrow clothes from. Through Skype dates that replace family dinners and snail mail that feels like a warm hug, we celebrate the unbreakable bonds of sisterhood. It's clear: in the grand sitcom of life, friends are the special guest stars who become series regulars, proving that sometimes, the best families are the ones we make, complete with their own blooper reels and spin-offs.

# CHAPTER 4

# Unwinding: A Guide to Wine and Whimsy

Ah, the quest to decipher your wine preferences and life's peculiarities resembles a whimsical odyssey, brimming with mishaps, giggles, and the occasional overzealous selections. But isn't that what makes the journey so delightful? Embracing the motto "It's wine o'clock somewhere" becomes your rallying cry, a gentle nudge to revel in moments of introspection and extravagance sans explanation. And amidst the swirls and sips, you come to realize that wine tasting transcends mere descriptors of oak or whispers of berries; it's a masterclass in mindfulness, a celebration of the present moment—one splendid glass after another. So, chin-chin to the art of savoring life, where every sip is a toast to being gloriously present, one sip at a time! Cheers to that!

## Red, White, and You: Understanding Your Taste in Wine and in Life

Navigating the vast universe of wines can feel like trying to wrangle a herd of tipsy cats—chaotic, amusing, and occasionally perplexing. But fear not, you need not be a wine whisperer to grasp the basics of this fermented grape extravaganza! Picture this: grapes, those noble fruit orbs, undergo a transformational journey involving squishing, fermenting, and voila!—wine is born. Some wines strut their stuff under varietal names like Pinot Noir, while others boast of their origins like a proud Burgundy. It's like naming your child after their personality or their birthplace, only with more fermenting involved.

Now, about those colors! Red wines, akin to their rebellious spirit, soak up the skins of dark grapes, while white wines prefer to shed their skins, opting for a lighter, more ethereal hue. Sweet wines? Well, they're the unapologetically sugary delights of the wine world, leaving a lingering sweetness like a mischievous wink. On the flip side, dry wines are like the stone-faced comedians of the bunch, leaving no sugar unfermented, offering a crisp, no-nonsense flavor.

But wait, there's more to this wine rodeo! Body, my dear oenophile, is not just about physique but about presence—the heavyweight contenders boasting intricate layers versus the lightweights, breezing through like a summer zephyr. And let's not forget the acidity, a zesty character trait that adds a refreshing twist, akin to a fruit basket tumbling into your glass.

Embarking on the delightful journey through the world of wines is akin to setting sail on a whimsical voyage, filled with tantalizing flavors and intriguing nuances waiting to be discovered. Here, amidst the vineyards and cellar doors, you'll encounter an array of varietals and blends, each with its own story to tell and secrets to unveil. Let's uncork the adventure with a few guiding stars (Hardin, 2020):

### *Types of White Wine*

- **Chardonnay:** Dry with hints of apple, citrus, and tropical fruits, and a medium-bodied profile.

- **Pinot Grigio/Gris:** Off-dry, featuring delicate fruit notes like peach and citrus, and a light to medium-bodied structure.

- **Riesling:** Ranging from off-dry to sweet, offering fruity notes of green apple and lime, and a light-bodied texture.

- **Sauvignon Blanc:** Off-dry and acidic, showcasing fresh green fruity flavors, and a light to medium-bodied feel.

- **Moscato (Muscat Blanc):** Sweet and juicy, bursting with fruity flavors, and light-bodied.

## *Types of Red Wine*

- **Cabernet Sauvignon:** Dry and full-bodied, with robust flavors of black cherry and black currant.

- **Pinot Noir:** Off-dry, displaying flavors of cherry and raspberry, with a light to medium-bodied character.

- **Merlot:** Dry, offering a blend of black cherry and chocolate notes, in a medium to full-bodied style.

- **Malbec:** Dry and full-bodied, boasting dark fruit and chocolate flavors.

- **Zinfandel:** Off-dry, presenting berry and fruit flavors, with a medium to full-body and high alcohol content.

- **Syrah:** Dry and full-bodied, featuring blueberry, plum, and chocolate notes.

Understanding the differences between red and white wines offers a captivating glimpse into the diverse world of oenology. Red wines, born from grapes with dark skins, unveil deep, rich hues, contrasting with the lighter appearance of whites, crafted from green-skinned grapes. As time's gentle caress weaves its magic, red wines, with their robust tannins, mature gracefully, fostering intricate layers of flavor and complexity, while whites maintain a youthful vibrancy. In the realm of body and character, reds reign supreme, boasting a lavish richness and boldness, while whites exude a refreshing lightness, akin to a gentle breeze on a summer day. Delving into the flavor palette, reds dazzle with their opulent display of dark fruit nuances, occasionally punctuated by whispers of chocolate or vanilla, while whites dance delicately across the palate with notes of crisp apple, zesty citrus, or fragrant florals. In the realm of alcohol content, reds typically wield a higher potency, adding a warm embrace to each sip, whereas whites offer a more restrained allure. As for serving temperature, reds thrive in the cozy embrace of room temperature, allowing their complexities to unfold, while whites revel in the crisp chill, accentuating their vibrant flavors. So, whether it's the sultry depths of a merlot or the refreshing tang of a sauvignon blanc, each wine tells a story, inviting you to savor every sip and explore the endless nuances of the vinicultural landscape. Cheers to the delightful journey of discovery!

So, armed with these insights, set forth on your wine-tasting adventure with enthusiasm and curiosity. Each glass holds a treasure trove of flavors waiting to be explored. Cheers to the journey ahead!

## "It's Wine O'Clock Somewhere": The Perfect Timing for a Glass of Self-Reflection

As we navigate the twists and turns of our daily journey, from the sunrise's gentle embrace to the moon's enchanting glow, wine accompanies us like a loyal companion, offering solace, joy, and moments of delightful introspection. In this delightful odyssey, the notion of the "perfect" time to indulge in a glass of wine becomes not merely a matter of ticking off boxes on a schedule, but rather an invitation to embrace the spontaneity and whimsy of life's fleeting moments.

Consider, if you will, the whimsical notion of a morning mimosa—a playful symphony of citrus and bubbles to greet the dawn. In the soft light of the rising sun, as the world stirs from its slumber, there exists a magical hour when the day holds limitless promise and the air is filled with the scent of possibility. Here, amidst the morning hustle and bustle, a glass of sparkling wine becomes more than just a beverage; it is a toast to new beginnings, a celebration of life's infinite potential.

As the day unfolds and the sun climbs higher in the sky, so too does the palette of wine choices expand, offering a kaleidoscope of flavors to tantalize the senses. Picture yourself, perhaps, lounging on a sun-drenched terrace, a crisp rosé in hand—the epitome of summer sophistication. With each sip, you are transported to a sun-kissed vineyard, where the grapes ripen under the golden rays of the sun, and the air is filled with the heady scent of blossoms and berries. Here, amidst the laughter of friends and the gentle hum of conversation, wine becomes more than just a drink; it is a gateway to shared moments of joy and camaraderie—a reminder that life's greatest pleasures are meant to be savored together.

But let us not forget the enchanting allure of the evening—the bewitching hour when the world slows down, and the stars twinkle mischievously in the night sky. Here, in the soft glow of candlelight, a glass of velvety red becomes more than just a beverage; it is a companion for moments of quiet introspection, a confidant in a world of swirling thoughts and fleeting emotions. As the wine dances across your palate, each sip becomes a journey—a voyage of discovery into the depths of your own soul.

In this enchanted hour, as the cares of the day melt away and the mysteries of the night unfold, wine becomes a conduit for self-reflection—a mirror to our deepest desires, fears, and aspirations. With each glass, we peel back the layers of our own humanity, exploring the tangled web of emotions and experiences that make us who we are. Here, amidst the flickering shadows and the soft murmur of conversation, we find solace in the simple act of being—of existing in this moment, in this place, with nothing but the gentle embrace of wine to guide us.

So, dear single woman, as you journey through the whimsical landscape of life, remember that the perfect time to drink a glass of wine is not found in the ticking of a clock or the pages of a calendar, but in the beating of your own heart, in the whispers of your own soul. Whether it is the dawn of a new day or the twilight of an old one, seize the opportunity to savor the simple pleasures and toast to the beauty of life's delightful absurdity. After all, in a world filled with chaos and uncertainty, a little wine and laughter go a long way. Cheers to that!

# The Zen of Wine Tasting: Learning to Savour the Moment, One Sip at a Time

Embarking on the journey of wine tasting is akin to stepping into a world of sensory delight—a realm where each swirl, sniff, and sip reveals layers of complexity and nuance waiting to be explored. Whether you're a seasoned connoisseur or a curious novice, there's always something new to discover in the vast landscape of wine.

At the heart of this exploration lies the art of savoring each sip, a practice that requires patience, mindfulness, and a keen sense of observation. For the single lady venturing into the world of wine tasting, this journey offers not only the opportunity to refine her palate but also a chance to connect with herself on a deeper level.

Let's delve into some key tips that can enhance the wine tasting experience and awaken the senses to the wonders of the grape.

- **The Power of Glassware:** It's often said that the right glass can make all the difference when it comes to enjoying wine. While you don't need to invest in an extensive collection of premium crystal stemware, choosing the appropriate glass for your wine can significantly enhance its aroma and flavor. For example, a larger bowl is ideal for red wines, allowing them to aerate and release their bouquet, while a smaller, narrower glass is better suited for white wines, preserving their delicate aromatics.

- **Temperature Matters:** Just as with other beverages, serving wine at the right temperature can greatly impact its taste and aroma. While red wines are typically served slightly below room temperature, around 60-65°F (15.56-18.33°C), white wines are best enjoyed chilled, between 45-55°F (7.22-12.78°C). This ensures that the wine's flavors are balanced and harmonious, without being overshadowed by extremes of temperature.

- **The Art of Decanting:** Decanting is a time-honored practice that allows wine to breathe, softening harsh tannins and enhancing its overall flavor profile. While it may seem like a daunting task, decanting can be as simple as pouring the wine into a glass pitcher or using a wine aerator for a quicker result. This process not only improves the wine's taste but also adds an element of theater to the tasting experience.

- **Navigating Wine Faults:** It's not uncommon to encounter wine faults, especially when dealing with more affordable options. One of the most recognizable faults is the presence of off-putting aromas, such as those resembling rotten eggs or cooked garlic. While these smells may be off-putting, they're often caused by yeast not receiving enough nutrients during fermentation, rather than indicating spoilage. Decanting these wines can help mitigate these unpleasant aromas, making them more palatable.

- **The Importance of Self-Reflection:** Beyond the technical aspects of wine tasting lies a deeper opportunity for self-reflection. As you engage with each glass of wine, take a moment to tune into your senses and observe the thoughts and emotions that arise. Notice how different wines make you feel, both physically and emotionally, and consider how these sensations relate to your personal preferences and experiences.

- **Exploring Pairings:** Wine tasting isn't just about the wine itself; it's also about the experience of pairing it with food. Experiment with different flavor combinations, from classic cheese and charcuterie boards to unexpected pairings like chocolate and wine. Pay attention to how the flavors interact and complement each other, and let your palate guide you in discovering new and exciting combinations.

- **Embracing the Journey:** Above all, remember that wine tasting is a journey, not a destination. Approach each tasting with an open mind and a sense of curiosity, and don't be afraid to explore outside your comfort zone. Whether you're sampling a familiar favorite or trying something completely new, embrace the adventure and allow yourself to be fully present in the moment.

The journey of wine tasting offers a rich tapestry of experiences, from the sensory delights of aroma and flavor to the deeper realms of self-discovery and reflection. By following these tips and embracing the spirit of exploration, the single lady can embark on a journey of palate enlightenment, one sip at a time. So raise your glass, savor the moment, and let the adventure begin! Cheers!

In conclusion, let your wine tasting exploration be guided by these questions. Are you team sweet or dry? Do you prefer the light, fruity dance or the richness of bold flavors? Is tartness your jam, or are you all about that smooth ride? Full-bodied or light and breezy? And last but not least, what aromas and flavor notes make your taste buds sing, and which ones have them saying 'No, thank you!'? Let these queries be your trusty compass as you navigate the delightful maze of wine tasting.

And there you have it, folks! Whether you're pondering the mysteries of life over a glass of merlot or embracing the zen of wine tasting with a crisp chardonnay, remember: it's always wine o'clock somewhere! So let's raise our glasses to the delightful journey of self-reflection, one sip at a time. May your wine be as rich as your experiences, as smooth as your conversations, and as bubbly as your laughter. Cheers to the reds, the whites, and to you—because when it comes to life and wine, there's always a reason to celebrate!

# CHAPTER 5

# The Economics of Being Eternally Single

We're about to uncover the mystical art form where managing finances isn't just about numbers on a spreadsheet—it's a dance of joy, a symphony of fiscal finesse that would make even the most stoic accountant break into a spontaneous jig.

Picture this: while others tremble at the mere mention of budgeting, we single souls embrace it with gusto, turning mundane money management into a thrilling quest for financial enlightenment. Who needs a partner when you have compound interest as your faithful companion and credit scores as your trusty steed?

But wait, there's more! In this whimsical land of solo finance, we discover that investing in experiences isn't just a line item in the budget—it's a gateway to a treasure trove of memories, where the ROI (Return on Investment) isn't measured in dollars but in laughter, learning, and a lifetime supply of epic tales.

Let's not overlook the hidden treasures of singlehood—the secret savings that come with the territory. Oh, the freedom! The freedom to jet off on spontaneous escapades, to treat ourselves to the finest of wines without a shadow of guilt looming over our heads. In this realm, buyer's remorse is but a myth, vanquished by the mighty sword of self-indulgence.

# Solo Budgeting 101: Managing Finances Without Compromising on Fun

Navigating the wild waters of personal finance as a singleton can be both liberating and daunting. On the one hand, you're the captain of your financial ship, steering it through the budgetary seas without needing to consult a first mate. Yet, on the other hand, you lack the safety net of a co-captain's income to cushion you from financial storms. Fear not, intrepid budgeter! With a dash of discipline and a sprinkle of savvy, you can chart a course toward financial stability without sacrificing an ounce of fun.

Let's start with the basics: budgeting. Picture it as the treasure map leading you to the fabled land of fiscal freedom. One popular route is the 50/30/20 method, where you allocate 50% of your booty for fixed costs, 20% for burying treasures (savings and debt repayment), and the remaining 30% for indulging in life's pleasures. While these percentages are like constellations guiding your financial ship, feel free to adjust them to suit your own treasure trove.

Ah, impulse shopping—the siren song that tempts many a budgeting sailor to veer off course. But fear not! Before you drop anchor on that shiny new purchase, heed the wise advice of waiting 48 hours. Use this time to consult your financial compass, weighing the pros and cons of your potential plunder. After all, a savvy sailor knows that delayed gratification can often lead to greater treasures down the line.

Now, let's talk sustenance. While the call of takeout may be strong, don't let it lure you into the Bermuda Triangle of overspending. Embrace the culinary arts and cook your own meals whenever possible. Bulk cooking becomes your first mate, saving you both doubloons and time throughout the week.

But what about your financial horizon? As you set sail toward future prosperity, don't forget to keep an eye on the horizon. Pay off any pesky debts that threaten to keelhaul your financial plans, even if they seem as harmless as a gentle breeze. And remember, wise spending isn't just about hoarding treasure—it's about investing in experiences that enrich your journey.

Yes, you heard right! In this budgeting adventure, experiences reign supreme. Explore new lands, try new activities, and push the boundaries of your comfort zone. For it's not the doubloons in your chest that bring true happiness, but the memories you collect along the way. So, set sail for the shores of joy and let your adventures be the compass guiding your spending decisions.

As you climb the ranks of your career and plunder greater treasures, don't be swayed by the allure of frivolous upgrades. Choose investments that enrich your life and align with your true compass heading. Whether it's upgrading your travel accommodations or adorning yourself with treasures that reflect your inner pirate, let your spending be a reflection of your values and passions.

And finally, remember this: while it's important to plan for the future, don't let the fear of tomorrow rob you of the joys of today. Embrace the balance between fiscal responsibility and living in the moment, for it is in this delicate dance that true financial freedom is found. So, hoist the sails, chart your course, and may your financial journey be as thrilling as a swashbuckling adventure on the high seas!

## Investing in Experiences, Not Just Assets: Building a Portfolio of Memories

In the adventurous journey of life, particularly as a single woman, there's a treasure trove of opportunities to invest in, experiences that enrich your soul and carve out a life brimming with joy and fulfillment.

Investing in experiences isn't just about creating fleeting moments of happiness—it's about building a rich tapestry of memories that sustain and nourish you throughout your life's journey. So, seize every opportunity to explore, learn, grow, and savor the beauty of the world around you, for these are the treasures that truly enrich the human experience.

## *Pursue Passionate Hobbies*

As a single woman, you have the luxury of time and freedom to explore your passions without external pressure. Whether it's painting vibrant canvases, penning eloquent prose, experimenting with culinary creations, or delving into any other creative pursuit, these hobbies aren't just pastimes—they're investments in your well-being. They provide avenues for self-expression, creativity, and personal fulfillment, enriching your life in ways that material possessions cannot. So, make it a priority to indulge in activities that spark joy and ignite your soul.

## *Cultivate Strong Friendships*

Friends are the family we choose for ourselves, and as a single woman, they play an invaluable role in providing support, companionship, and laughter along life's journey. Invest time and effort in nurturing these relationships, whether it's through regular get-togethers, heartfelt conversations, or shared experiences. Surround yourself with people who uplift and inspire you, and cherish the bonds that transcend distance and time. Remember, friendships are not just a source of joy—they're a vital aspect of emotional well-being.

## *Prioritize Self-Care*

In the hustle and bustle of everyday life, it's easy to neglect self-care in favor of meeting external obligations. However, as a single woman, taking care of your physical, emotional, and mental health is paramount. Make it a priority to nourish your body with nutritious food, engage in regular exercise, prioritize quality sleep, and practice mindfulness to cultivate inner peace and resilience. Remember, self-care isn't selfish—it's essential for your overall well-being and ability to thrive.

### *Embrace Spontaneity and Adventure*

Being single affords you the freedom to be spontaneous and adventurous, so seize the opportunity to explore new horizons and embrace life's unpredictability. Whether it's embarking on solo travels to far-off destinations, immersing yourself in local cultural experiences, or trying your hand at adrenaline-pumping activities, be open to new possibilities and step outside your comfort zone. Embracing spontaneity fosters personal growth, expands your horizons, and creates lasting memories that enrich your life.

### *Set Boundaries*

As a single woman, it's essential to set boundaries to protect your time, energy, and emotional well-being. Know your limits and communicate them clearly with others, whether it's in your personal or professional life. Learn to say no to commitments that don't align with your priorities or values, and prioritize activities that bring you joy and fulfillment. Setting boundaries empowers you to maintain a healthy balance and focus on what truly matters to you.

### *Continuous Learning and Growth*

Investing in your education and personal development is a lifelong journey that enriches your mind and expands your horizons. Whether it's through formal education, online courses, workshops, or self-directed learning, prioritize opportunities for growth and self-improvement. Stay curious, embrace new challenges, and never stop seeking knowledge and experiences that enrich your life and deepen your understanding of the world around you.

### *Utilize Valuable Resources*

In today's digital age, a wealth of learning opportunities is just a click away. Take advantage of podcasts, online articles, YouTube videos, and online courses to expand your knowledge and skills. Attend events, workshops, and webinars to gain insights from experts in various fields and connect with like-minded individuals. These valuable resources provide endless opportunities for learning, growth, and personal development.

### Invest in Personal Development

Enhancing essential skills such as self-confidence, leadership, digital literacy, and communication is key to personal and professional success. Seek out workshops, courses, and mentorship opportunities to develop these skills and unlock your full potential. Whether it's honing your public speaking abilities, refining your leadership skills, or mastering new technologies, investing in personal development empowers you to thrive in all aspects of your life.

### Learn From Mentors

Mentorship is a powerful tool for personal and professional growth, providing guidance, support, and valuable insights from experienced individuals. Seek out mentors in your field or industry and learn from their wisdom and experience. Reach out for coffee chats, informational interviews, or mentorship programs to cultivate meaningful connections. Engage in open and honest conversations, asking for advice, feedback, and constructive criticism. Be proactive in seeking out mentorship opportunities and demonstrate your willingness to learn and grow. Remember, mentorship is a two-way street—be respectful of your mentor's time and expertise, and be grateful for the knowledge and guidance they impart. By fostering mentorship relationships, you can accelerate your personal and professional development and gain valuable insights that will shape your journey towards success.

### Cultivate Quiet Reflection

In the midst of life's hustle and bustle, it's crucial to carve out moments of quiet reflection to connect with your inner self and gain clarity on your goals and aspirations. Create space for solitude and contemplation, whether it's through daily meditation, journaling, or spending time in nature. Disconnect from distractions and allow yourself to be fully present in the moment, embracing the stillness and serenity that come with quiet introspection. Use these moments to reflect on your values, aspirations, and the path you want to chart for your life. By cultivating a practice of quiet reflection, you can gain insight, perspective, and inner peace amidst life's whirlwind.

Investing in experiences as a single woman goes far beyond acquiring material possessions or building financial wealth. It's about nurturing relationships, prioritizing self-care, embracing adventure, and fostering personal growth and development. By prioritizing experiences that enrich your life and deepen your understanding of yourself and the world around you, you can create a portfolio of memories that bring joy, fulfillment, and meaning to your life's journey. So, seize every opportunity to explore, learn, grow, and savor the beauty of life, for these are the treasures that truly enrich the human experience.

## The Secret Savings of Singlehood: Embracing the Financial Freedoms of Flying Solo

In the vast sea of financial advice, one beacon shines particularly bright for individuals navigating the waters solo: save, save, save! While the absence of a dual income may seem daunting at times, it also presents an opportunity for you to take control of your financial future like never before. Here's why saving money should be your compass in these uncharted waters:

1. **Build Your Safety Net:** Without the luxury of a second income to fall back on, having a substantial emergency fund becomes your lifeline. Aim to save enough to cover at least six months of expenses. While it may seem excessive, this cushion can shield you from unexpected job loss or surprise expenses, ensuring you stay afloat even in the stormiest of financial seas.

2. **Tackle High-Interest Debt:** Not all debts are created equal, but high-interest debts can be anchors dragging down your financial

progress. Prioritize paying off debts with the highest interest rates first. By freeing yourself from the burden of debt, you'll pave the way for smoother sailing towards your larger financial goals.

3.   **Invest in Your Future:** Retirement may seem like a distant island on the horizon, but the sooner you start sailing toward it, the better. Take advantage of any employer-sponsored retirement accounts available to you, especially if they offer matching contributions. Maximize your contributions each year and familiarize yourself with the IRS rules (or whatever rules prevail in your jurisdiction) to ensure you're making the most of your retirement savings potential.

4.   **Diversify Your Investments:** Just as a skilled captain spreads their cargo across different compartments of the ship, diversifying your investments minimizes risk and maximizes returns. Split your investments between stocks, bonds, and other assets, tailoring your portfolio to fit your risk tolerance and time horizon.

5.   **Protect Your Future:** While it's not always pleasant to think about, safeguarding your health and financial well-being is crucial. Consider long-term care insurance, especially as women tend to live longer and face higher rates of chronic health issues. Additionally, explore life insurance options to cover debts and final expenses, ensuring your loved ones aren't burdened in the event of the unexpected.

6.   **Plan Your Legacy:** Estate planning may seem like uncharted territory, but it's essential for ensuring your assets are distributed according to your wishes. Regardless of your marital status or parental responsibilities, crafting a comprehensive estate plan ensures your legacy is preserved and your loved ones are cared for.

7.   **Choose Your Allies:** In the absence of a spouse, it's crucial to designate trusted individuals to make healthcare and financial decisions on your behalf if you're unable to do so yourself.

Establishing powers of attorney and executing a will may seem daunting, but doing so ensures you're prepared for whatever may lie ahead.

While it may be tempting to sail through life without a financial roadmap, taking control of your finances and prioritizing savings is the compass that will guide you toward a brighter, more secure future. By heeding this advice and charting a course toward financial independence, you'll navigate the seas of singlehood with confidence and resilience.

Remember this: managing your finances doesn't have to be a dull affair devoid of fun and excitement. Instead, it's an opportunity to craft a life that's both financially sound and endlessly fulfilling. By embracing the principles of solo budgeting, investing in experiences, and reveling in the secret savings of singlehood, you've unlocked the door to a world where financial freedom and fun coexist harmoniously. So, as you navigate the seas of life, may you continue to chart your course with confidence, knowing that you have the skills and knowledge to steer toward a bright and prosperous future.

Whether you're setting sail on a new financial adventure or basking in the memories of past experiences, always remember to cherish the journey and celebrate the small victories along the way. After all, life is too short to let worries about money dampen your spirits. So, here's to embracing the joys of solo budgeting, building a portfolio of memories that will last a lifetime, and reveling in the freedom and independence of flying solo. May your sails be full, your pockets be plentiful, and your adventures be endless.

# CHAPTER 6

# Yoga Pants: The New Business Casual

Once upon a time, in the majestic realm of comfort, where couches were thrones and slippers were crowns, there existed a magical garment that reigned supreme: yoga pants. Yes, in this kingdom, stretchy fabric and flexible waistbands held more power than any scepter or royal decree. But this chapter isn't just about lounging around in downward dog. Oh no, it's a celebration—a grand fiesta, if you will—of the extraordinary evolution of activewear into a bonafide fashion phenomenon. It's as if the yoga studio and the catwalk had a lovechild, and that lovechild decided to strut its stuff right down the street.

So here's to the bold proclamation that feeling good is the new looking good, and to the audacious souls who dare to ask the age-old question: "Do these yoga pants make my aura look big?" Well, spoiler alert, darlings: not only do they make it look big, they make it look positively fabulous! In a world where body positivity reigns supreme and comfort is king, these yoga pants aren't just a garment—they're a manifesto. So grab your stretchiest pair, strike a pose, and let's embark on this stylishly comfortable adventure together. Namaste, fabulous beings. Namaste.

## From Studio to Street: Making Activewear Your Everyday Wear

Embarking on a regular yoga practice isn't just about physical exertion—it's a journey toward inner peace, clarity, and self-awareness. These qualities cultivated on the mat have a curious way of seeping into other aspects of our lives, shaping how we navigate the world beyond the confines of the yoga studio. But what's equally fascinating is how the clothing we wear during our practice seamlessly integrates into our everyday wardrobe, blurring the lines between activewear and fashion.

Yoga activewear, once reserved solely for the studio, has now transcended its boundaries to become a staple in everyday fashion. This shift, often referred to as the rise of athleisure, has revolutionized how we approach dressing for comfort without compromising on style. Gone are the days when activewear was confined to the gym—it's now a versatile and chic option for women seeking both comfort and fashion, whether they're running errands, meeting friends for brunch, or enjoying a night out on the town.

So how exactly can we take our trusty yoga wear and transform it into fashion-forward outfits fit for any occasion? Let's explore some practical yet stylish tips:

· **Layer With a Jacket**: A key strategy for elevating your yoga attire into streetwear chic is layering. A casual jacket serves as a versatile piece that instantly adds sophistication to any activewear ensemble. Whether it's a denim jacket for a laid-back vibe, a bomber jacket for an edgy touch, or a cozy cardigan for those chilly days, layering allows you to play with textures and proportions, adding depth and interest to your outfit.

· **Tie a Knot in Your Tank**: While loose and lightweight tanks are perfect for intense yoga sessions, they can also be styled for everyday wear with a simple trick: tying a knot. By cinching the fabric at the bottom into a side or center knot, you instantly create a more tailored and fashion-forward silhouette. This effortless accessory adds a touch of personality to your gym tank, making it suitable for casual outings without sacrificing comfort.

· **Pair With a Stylish Graphic Tee or Slogan Top**: Add some personality to your yoga pants ensemble by pairing them with a trendy graphic tee or a top featuring a catchy slogan or inspiring message. Opt for bold prints, quirky graphics, or vintage-inspired designs to inject a playful and fashionable element into your look. Tying the tee at the waist or opting for a cropped style can also create a more flattering silhouette. This effortless pairing of yoga pants with a stylish top allows you to express your individuality while staying comfortable and chic on the streets.

- **Throw on an Oversized Sweater:** For an effortlessly chic look that seamlessly transitions from the yoga studio to the streets, consider pairing your favorite leggings with an oversized sweater. Not only does this combination exude the latest trends in boho-chic fashion, but it also offers unparalleled comfort. To elevate the look further, add ankle boots and opt for a casual hairstyle like a top knot—perfect for a day of leisurely activities or casual meetups with friends.

- **It's All in the Details:** Accessories play a pivotal role in transforming your yoga-inspired ensemble into a fashion statement. Whether it's long necklaces, silver or gold bangles, or accent rings, the right accessories can elevate your look from gym casual to street style chic. Choose footwear that complements your outfit—sneakers for a sporty vibe or boots for a more polished appearance. And don't underestimate the power of a well-styled hairstyle—whether it's a messy braid, a sleek ponytail, or tousled waves, your hair can add the finishing touch to your overall look.

In essence, the seamless integration of yoga activewear into everyday fashion represents a celebration of versatility and empowerment. It's a testament to the modern woman's desire to balance comfort with style, allowing her to move seamlessly between different facets of her life with confidence and grace. So the next time you reach for your trusty pair of leggings or your favorite yoga tank, remember that you're not just dressing for the studio—you're creating a fashion statement that effortlessly transcends boundaries and reflects your unique sense of style.

# The Philosophy of Comfort: Why Feeling Good is the New Looking Good

In the intricate dance between feeling good and looking good, there lies a profound truth: true beauty radiates from within. Yet, in a world fixated on external appearances, this sentiment often gets lost in the cacophony of societal standards and superficial expectations. How many times have we witnessed someone physically attractive lamenting their inner turmoil, only to be met with incredulous stares? It's a paradoxical notion, one that prompts us to reconsider the essence of true beauty.

Looking good, as it turns out, encompasses far more than just superficial aesthetics. It's a reflection of our innermost thoughts, emotions, and self-perception—a mirror through which our inner radiance shines forth for the world to behold.

Consider a day when everything seems to fall effortlessly into place—your mood is buoyant, your decisions are clear, and your interactions are imbued with positivity. Notice how others respond to this aura of contentment and confidence that envelops you. Even amidst the chaos of external circumstances, your inner stability remains unwavering, shielding you from the influence of negativity.

In this delicate balance between feeling good and looking good, it becomes evident that prioritizing inner well-being is paramount. For while external appearances may temporarily gratify the senses, it is the cultivation of inner peace and self-love that fosters lasting fulfillment and genuine beauty.

So where does one begin on the journey to feeling good from within? The answer lies in nurturing a holistic sense of well-being—one that encompasses the physical, mental, and emotional dimensions of our existence. First and foremost, physical health forms the cornerstone of our overall well-being. It's not merely about adhering to societal standards of beauty, but rather, it's about honoring our bodies as temples of vitality and resilience. This begins with conscious choices regarding nutrition and exercise—a commitment to nourishing our bodies with wholesome foods and engaging in regular physical activity.

Consider the transformative power of simple dietary changes—a shift from processed foods laden with artificial sugars and preservatives to nutrient-rich alternatives that fuel our bodies with vitality. By prioritizing whole foods and embracing mindful eating habits, we lay the foundation for optimal physical health and vitality.

Similarly, regular exercise serves as a cornerstone of our physical well-being, not only strengthening our bodies but also uplifting our spirits. The endorphin release that accompanies a vigorous workout invigorates the mind and uplifts the soul, infusing us with a sense of euphoria and empowerment.

Moreover, cultivating healthy habits throughout our daily routine further enhances our overall well-being. From prioritizing adequate sleep to practicing mindfulness and stress-reduction techniques, every conscious choice we make contributes to our inner equilibrium.

Yet, perhaps the most profound transformation occurs within the realm of self-perception and emotional well-being. Learning to embrace ourselves with unconditional love and acceptance is the ultimate act of self-care—a journey toward profound self-discovery and inner fulfillment.

In a society that often perpetuates unrealistic beauty standards and fosters self-doubt, practicing self-love becomes a revolutionary act—one that challenges the status quo and empowers us to reclaim our inherent worthiness. It's about celebrating our unique quirks and imperfections, recognizing that true beauty transcends physical appearance and emanates from the depths of our souls.

Indeed, the path to feeling good from within is paved with self-compassion, gratitude, and authenticity. It's about honoring our intrinsic value as human beings and embracing the full spectrum of our emotions, both light and shadow.

So the next time you find yourself caught in the relentless pursuit of external validation, pause and remember: true beauty begins within. By nurturing our inner radiance and cultivating a sense of well-being that transcends superficial appearances, we embark on a journey of self-discovery and empowerment—a journey toward unparalleled beauty that radiates from the depths of our souls.

## "Do These Yoga Pants Make My Aura Look Big?": Embracing Body Positivity

In a world where beauty standards seem to dictate our worth, navigating the path toward self-acceptance can feel like a daunting journey. The constant barrage of images and messages promoting unrealistic ideals often leads to self-criticism and feelings of inadequacy. However, amidst this cultural landscape, the philosophy of body positivity emerges as a beacon of hope—a guiding light that empowers individuals to forge a compassionate connection with their bodies, irrespective of size, shape, or appearance.

At its core, body positivity advocates for a mindset shift—one that transcends societal dictates and embraces the inherent worth and beauty of every individual. It is a call to arms against the relentless pursuit of perfection and a celebration of diversity in all its forms. By fostering self-acceptance, promoting self-confidence, and challenging societal norms, body positivity seeks to liberate individuals from the shackles of unrealistic beauty standards.

This comprehensive guide is designed to offer practical strategies and transformative practices aimed at nurturing body positivity and fostering a deep sense of self-love and acceptance. Through self-reflection, mindful self-care, the cultivation of self-esteem, and the cultivation of supportive communities, individuals can embark on a journey toward complete body acceptance.

Self-reflection serves as a powerful tool in the quest for body positivity, providing a gateway to increased self-awareness and understanding. By examining our thoughts, beliefs, and attitudes toward our bodies, we gain insight into the internalized messages that shape our self-perception. Acknowledging negative thoughts and challenging unrealistic standards are crucial first steps toward cultivating a more positive body image.

Furthermore, understanding triggers and empowering oneself to define beauty on one's own terms are essential components of self-reflection. By recognizing and avoiding triggers that exacerbate self-esteem concerns, individuals can create a supportive environment conducive to body positivity. Additionally, reclaiming agency over beauty standards and rejecting societal norms empowers individuals to embrace their bodies with confidence and pride.

In addition to self-reflection, nurturing mental and emotional well-being is paramount for cultivating body positivity. Practices such as self-compassion, mindfulness, creative expression, and social connection are integral components of a holistic approach to self-care. By extending kindness and understanding to oneself, engaging in mindfulness exercises, expressing emotions through creative outlets, and fostering meaningful relationships, individuals can cultivate a deep sense of inner peace and fulfillment.

Moreover, immersing oneself in body-positive media resources offers an alternative narrative to the pervasive messages of mainstream media. By consuming content that celebrates diversity, authenticity, and self-acceptance, individuals can counteract the harmful effects of unrealistic beauty standards and reaffirm their commitment to body positivity.

When it comes to physical health, prioritizing practices that honor the body and promote overall well-being is essential. Gratitude journaling, quality sleep, stress management, balanced nutrition, and joyful movement are all integral components of a healthy lifestyle rooted in self-love and self-care. By nourishing the body with wholesome foods, prioritizing rest and relaxation, and engaging in activities that bring joy and vitality, individuals can honor their bodies as sacred vessels of life and vitality.

Building self-esteem is another crucial aspect of nurturing body positivity. By celebrating achievements, challenging limiting beliefs, engaging in personal growth, setting boundaries, and fostering connections with supportive communities, individuals can cultivate a strong sense of self-worth and confidence. Recognizing and celebrating one's unique strengths and talents, setting achievable goals, and seeking out opportunities for personal development are all effective strategies for enhancing self-esteem and promoting body positivity.

Finally, finding a supportive community of like-minded individuals can provide invaluable encouragement and validation on the journey toward body positivity. Whether through online forums, social media groups, or local meet-ups, connecting with others who share similar experiences can foster a sense of belonging and empowerment. By sharing stories, offering support, and celebrating each other's successes, individuals can find strength and inspiration in community and realize that they are not alone in their journey toward self-love and acceptance.

In conclusion, nurturing body positivity is a transformative journey—one that requires courage, compassion, and commitment. By engaging in self-reflection, practicing mindful self-care, cultivating self-esteem, and seeking support from supportive communities, individuals can embark on a path toward complete body acceptance. Remember, true beauty lies not in conformity to external standards but in the unique essence of each individual. Embrace your body, honor your worth, and celebrate the beauty that is uniquely yours. You are enough, just as you are.

To all the single ladies out there, let's wrap up this chapter with a fabulous finale that'll leave you feeling empowered and ready to conquer the world in your activewear! From studio to street, we've unraveled the mysteries of activewear, proving that comfort is truly queen in the realm of fashion. Say goodbye to stiff jeans and suffocating skirts—now, you can strut your stuff in stretchy leggings and cozy hoodies, feeling as fabulous as you look.

In our quest to understand the philosophy of comfort, we've uncovered the divine truth: feeling good is the new looking good.

So why settle for anything less than clothes that make you feel like a million bucks? And as for embracing body positivity, well, let's just say we've mastered the art of loving ourselves, flaws and all. So the next time you ask yourself, "Do these yoga pants make my aura look big?" just remember: your aura is shining bright, baby, and those pants are just adding a little extra sparkle.

So here's to you, single ladies! Keep rocking those activewear ensembles, embracing the philosophy of comfort, and radiating body positivity wherever you go. Because when you feel good, you look even better—and that's a fact worth celebrating!

# CHAPTER 7

# Reading as a Radical Act of Self-Love

In the quietude that blankets the room, with only the soft whisper of turning pages for company, you embark upon a journey that is at once solitary and profoundly connected. It is in these serene moments, nestled between the comforting embrace of a book's pages, that a unique form of solace is found. Adventure beckons, not to distant lands, but inward, to the vast landscapes of the soul. Herein lies a love not shouted from the rooftops, but whispered in the quiet moments of understanding oneself. This chapter is an ode to that journey, an exploration of how stories serve as both a shelter from the storm and a mirror reflecting the intricate designs of our hearts.

Books, in their silent wisdom, offer hugs that wrap around us, warming the chill of solitude with their understanding embrace. They speak a language of empathy, saying without words, "I understand." It's in this sacred exchange that a book becomes more than just an assembly of printed words; it transforms into a companion, a mentor, and at times, a healer.

## Books That Hug Back: Finding Stories That Resonate With Your Soul

Ah, the age-old quest for the perfect book—akin to searching for a needle in a haystack, if the haystack were as big as the internet and the needle kept changing genres. Whether you're a bibliophile with a voracious appetite or a rookie reader making tentative steps into the literary jungle, fear not! The path to your next 5-star read is littered with amusing detours and serendipitous discoveries.

- **Embrace Your Author Crush:** Starting with the obvious—you've got an author crush, the kind that makes your heart flutter at the mere mention of their name. Delve into their lesser-known works; who knows, you might stumble upon a hidden gem that hasn't yet made it to the Instagram hall of fame. Imagine the bragging rights!

- **The Critics' Darlings:** Venture into the realm of critically acclaimed masterpieces. Yes, those tomes that everyone says you "must" read before you die. They're like the broccoli of the literary world: supposedly good for you, but you're not entirely sure you like them. Yet, every now and then, you find one that surprises you, kind of like discovering that broccoli can be delicious with the right seasoning.

- **Follow Your Hobby:** Next up, why not let your hobbies guide you? If you're into underwater basket weaving, there's probably a book about it, or at least one that features it in a chapter or two. This approach is like going on a blind date with a book that shares your interests. Sure, it might not end in true love, but at least you'll have something to talk about.

- **Phone a Sister:** Remember, the bookish community is vast and usually very friendly. Hit up your well-read friend, the one who actually uses their library card, and ask for recommendations. Or better yet, chat with the local bookseller who, by now, is probably on a first-name basis with every character in their store. It's like matchmaking but for readers.

- **Surf the Literary Waves:** Ah, the internet—a treasure trove of book reviews, recommendations, and debates about whether the movie was better (it usually isn't). Dive into the latest buzz, but be warned: this may lead to a TBR (To Be Read) list that's longer than your monthly grocery list.

- **Join the Club:** Book clubs: where books are sometimes read, wine is often consumed, and friendships are made. It's like group therapy but for book lovers. You might not adore every book, but you'll definitely have opinions, and that's half the fun.

- **Library Lottery:** Take a chance on your library's recommendations. It's a bit like playing the lottery, except instead of money, you win stories. Who knows? The next book you check out could be the one that changes your life, or at least keeps you entertained for a weekend.

- **Judge a Book by Its Cover (Sometimes):** Wander the aisles of a bookstore or library and let your intuition guide you. It's okay to judge books by their covers here; designers work hard on them for a reason! When something catches your eye, give it the good old back-cover blurb test. If it passes, congrats, you might have found your next read!

- **The First Chapter Rule:** The first chapter is like a first date: it doesn't have to be perfect, but you should at least want to see where things go. If the book hasn't captured your interest by then, it's okay to ghost it. There are plenty of other books in the sea.

- **Movie Magic:** Loved a movie? Chances are it was a book first. Hollywood's originality has been in question for years, so there's a high probability your favorite film was born from a book. This is your chance to be that person who says, "The book was better."

- **Six Degrees of Literary Separation:** Finally, dive into the inspirations behind your favorite stories. It's like playing six degrees of separation but with books. Your favorite author's favorite author could become your new obsession, leading you down a rabbit hole of literary bliss.

In the end, finding that perfect book may require a mix of strategy, serendipity, and sheer luck. But remember, in the grand adventure of reading, sometimes it's the journey that counts, not just the destination. So, happy book hunting! May your shelves overflow, and your reading nook always be cozy.

# The DIY Therapy Session: How Reading Can Be Your Personal Psychologist

In a world where scrolling through doom and gloom on the internet is a pastime, the act of cracking open a book might just be the unsung superhero of mental wellbeing. Imagine, if you will, a universe where books are akin to vitamins for the soul, and reading is the workout your brain craves for those deep, emotional gains. Welcome to the hilariously serious world of bibliotherapy!

Now, let's dive into the meat of the matter: Can reading truly spiffy up our mental health? Scientists, with their fancy studies and big words, say "Yes!" And who are we to argue? After all, diving into the pages of a good book allows us to slip into someone else's shoes, sprint a mile, and come back with newfound empathy, all without moving from our favorite reading nook.

The concept of narrative absorption, a term that sounds like what happens when you spill tea on your book, is actually the fancy way of saying that getting lost in a story is more than just a delightful pastime—it's a gateway to enhancing our sense of wellbeing. Picture yourself transported to the mystical lands of Middle-Earth, navigating the social labyrinths of Victorian England, or solving mysteries with a cup of tea in hand in a cozy English village. These mental vacations provide not only an escape but also a unique opportunity for introspection and contemplation.

Researchers, possibly in lab coats surrounded by stacks of novels, have found that when we read, parts of our brain light up like a Christmas tree—not just any parts, but specifically those involved in understanding others. This literary magic trick allows us to better grasp the complex web of human emotions and intentions. So, when Aunt Edna says she "just loves" your new fluorescent green hair, you might understand what's really going on beneath the surface.

The wonders of reading don't stop there. Books are like the slow-release capsules of the mental health world. The benefits linger, reducing symptoms of depression and even extending our lifespan.

Yes, you heard that right—devouring books might just help you dodge the Grim Reaper. Who knew that the secret to immortality was nestled between the pages of *War and Peace*?

In these pandemic times, where our social skills might be rustier than a knight's armor after a rainstorm, fiction offers a lifeline. It seems that getting emotionally entangled with fictional characters is not just for the overly dramatic; it's a proven way to boost empathy and social cognition. Essentially, reading about Elizabeth Bennet's romantic entanglements could help you navigate your own social quagmires.

Frequent fiction readers, it turns out, are not just folks with impressive bookshelves; they're likely to have better social skills. It's as if each novel is a level in the ultimate video game of human understanding, and every page turn levels you up. This might explain why bookworms often come across as wise sages, dispensing advice with a knowing look over the rims of their glasses.

But wait, there's more! For younglings navigating the stormy seas of adolescence, reading can act as a compass. It helps them understand the tumultuous nature of human emotions and find their place in the world. Through identifying with characters, readers learn they're not alone in their struggles, providing a comfort that sometimes real-life conversations fail to offer.

So, the next time someone questions your towering to-be-read pile, just tell them you're engaging in a highly sophisticated form of mental gymnastics and emotional resilience training. Whether you're leafing through the latest bestseller, a dusty classic, or even a graphic novel, you're not just reading—you're giving your brain a hug, expanding your empathy muscles, and maybe, just maybe, adding a tick to your lifespan.

In conclusion, if books were a medication, they'd be the kind with an overwhelmingly positive section on the side effects label: may cause increased empathy, improved social cognition, and an enhanced sense of wellbeing. Side effects include getting emotionally attached to fictional characters and an insatiable desire for just one more chapter. Proceed with caution, and happy reading!

# Read, Reflect, Repeat: The Cycle of Learning and Growing Through Literature

In the quiet hours of the morning, when the world still slumbers in the remnants of night's embrace, there exists a routine that is both simple and profoundly impactful. It belongs to a person who has discovered the secret garden of mindfulness and reflection, cultivated through the pages of books and the silent dialogue with one's own thoughts. This person, let's call them Alex, has embraced a ritual that starts with an hour of reading every morning, followed by a period of deep contemplation. This practice, seemingly mundane at first glance, has unfolded layers of clarity and awareness in Alex's life, proving to be a wellspring of personal growth and understanding.

Alex's journey into this ritualistic practice began almost inadvertently, a mere routine that gradually morphed into a cornerstone of their daily life. Reading, for Alex, is not just an activity but a voyage into the realms of knowledge, empathy, and insight. However, it's the act of pausing after this voyage, to reflect on the traversed paths, that has amplified the benefits manifold. This pause, ranging from five to ten minutes of deep contemplation, sometimes happens amidst morning chores, turning mundane tasks into moments of profound reflection. Other times, it's a stillness, a quiet staring at the walls, allowing the mind to wander through the corridors of newly acquired knowledge.

This habit of reflection has acted as a catalyst in making Alex more mindful of how time is spent. The awareness that comes from reflecting on the passage of time, on the actions undertaken, brings a clarity that is both liberating and empowering. It's a realization that managing time isn't just about scheduling and tasks but about understanding the value of each moment, and how it contributes to personal growth.

Similarly, Alex's approach to reading mirrors this mindfulness. By dedicating time to ponder over the read material, Alex engages in a process of reflective reading, which has become a critical component of their learning. This reflection isn't just a cursory glance back at the text but a deep, immersive process. Alex revisits the learned concepts, the narratives, and the underlying messages, allowing them to crystallize in the mind. It's a process of creating a vivid tapestry of knowledge, where each thread is examined, understood, and appreciated.

The act of reflection, for Alex, is akin to zooming out to grasp the bigger picture. It's about seeing the connections between disparate ideas, understanding the depth of characters, and appreciating the nuance of arguments. This panoramic view of knowledge isn't just about recall but about integrating these insights into one's worldview, making the act of reading a transformative experience.

The methodology is simple yet profound: Read. Reflect. Repeat. This cycle, ingrained in Alex's routine over the months, has become a testament to the power of consistency. Like the steady drip of water that wears away stone, this practice of reflective reading and contemplation has sculpted Alex's mind, making it more receptive, discerning, and at peace.

Alex's experience of reflective reading versus non-reflective reading has been revelatory. Reading without reflection feels like skimming the surface of a vast ocean, touching only the fleeting waves without ever plunging into the depths. In contrast, reflective reading, accompanied by contemplation, has allowed Alex to dive deep, to explore the mysteries and treasures hidden below the surface. It's a richer, more fulfilling experience that leaves Alex feeling content, at peace, and, more importantly, connected to the essence of the material.

This reflective practice has extended beyond the confines of reading. Random morning tasks, such as brushing teeth or folding bed sheets, become moments of recapitulation, where thoughts and learnings from the reading session meander through Alex's mind, further solidifying the insights gained. This continuous engagement with the material ensures that the knowledge doesn't just pass through but settles in, becoming a part of Alex's cognitive and emotional landscape.

In embracing this ritual of reading and reflection, Alex has discovered more than just a method of learning; they have found a pathway to mindfulness, a strategy for living a more conscious, aware, and fulfilling life. It's a testament to the idea that the act of reading, when coupled with reflection, can transcend the boundaries of entertainment or education, becoming a powerful tool for personal development and wellbeing.

Through this journey, Alex has not only expanded their mind but also enriched their soul, proving that in the quietude of reflection, the mind finds its most profound insights, and in the pages of a book, the heart finds its most profound connections.

Remember, the next time you're feeling lost, overwhelmed, or just in need of a little guidance, there's probably a book out there waiting to hug you back, to offer you the wisdom, comfort, and escape you need. Your personal psychologist doesn't necessarily have a medical degree but might just have a library card.

And now, for a final joke to close this chapter:

Why don't books ever get lonely? Because they always have their characters for company, and when they need a little extra love, they know there's someone out there who will hug them back—even if it's just on their bookshelf.

May your shelves always overflow with books that hug back, and may your journey through their pages bring you the peace, understanding, and joy you seek.

# CHAPTER 8

# The Sisterhood of the Traveling Wine Glasses

Step into a world where every sip unlocks a new adventure, where the clinking of glasses heralds the beginning of a journey spanning continents and cultures. Why wait for the elusive perfect moment to explore the world's vineyards when the world of wine awaits at your fingertips, right in the comfort of your living room? Picture this: surrounded by your closest companions, the sisterhood you've cultivated over time, as you uncork a bottle of French Bordeaux. With each velvety sip, let the flavors carry you away to the sun-drenched vineyards of France, where time slows and worries fade into the background.

But the journey doesn't end there. Oh no, it's just the beginning. Next week, it might be a Spanish Rioja that graces your palate, beckoning you to embrace the fiery passion of flamenco and the warmth of Spanish hospitality. The beauty of this global wine-tasting adventure lies not only in the diverse flavors that dance across your tongue but in the shared laughter and camaraderie that accompany each pour.

Indeed, traveling with your chosen sisters is akin to starring in your own live comedy show, where every mishap becomes a cherished memory in the grand tapestry of friendship. From impromptu wine tastings at the airport causing missed flights to navigating labyrinthine foreign cities armed with nothing but a map and a sense of adventure, the misadventures are as plentiful as the memories they create. But therein lies the magic—for it's not about avoiding the hiccups, but rather embracing them as part of the journey, to be recounted with fondness over glasses of wine for years to come.

Yet, the allure of cultural exploration extends beyond just wine. Enter the realm of cultural cocktails—each concoction a tantalizing blend of flavors and history, offering a glimpse into the soul of a nation with every sip. Picture yourself savoring a delicate Sake in Japan, the nuances of its taste echoing centuries of tradition and craftsmanship. Or perhaps it's a zesty Margarita in Mexico, the tang of lime and tequila sparking conversations about fiestas and folklore.

And let's not forget the quintessentially British Pimm's, a refreshing elixir that embodies the essence of a summer afternoon in merry old England. With each sip, delve deeper into the rich tapestry of cultures, traditions, and the stories behind the drinks we hold dear. It's more than just imbibing; it's a journey of growth and discovery, a celebration of the diversity that makes our world so vibrant.

So why wait for the perfect moment to explore? Grab a glass, gather your sisters, and embark on a global adventure from the comfort of your own home. After all, the world of wine and cocktails awaits, ready to transport you to far-off lands and ignite your thirst for discovery. Cheers to the journey ahead!

## Wine Tasting Around the World: From Your Living Room to the Vineyards of France

Embarking on a wine tasting journey promises to unveil a tapestry of unique experiences, each winery offering its own distinct charm and allure. Whether it's the variety of grapes cultivated, the picturesque landscapes, or the architectural marvels of the winery facilities, every stop along the way adds a new dimension to the adventure.

When it comes to exploring the world of wine, diversity is key. That's why it's recommended to visit several wineries during your tour. By doing so, you'll have the opportunity to immerse yourself in a range of tasting experiences, from sampling different wine styles amidst the vineyards to delving into the nuances of wine aging in the barrel rooms.

At a vineyard tasting, guests are warmly welcomed by the vintner who guides them through the winery's operations before leading them out to the vineyard itself. Here, amidst the rows of grapevines, visitors have the chance to taste a selection of wines crafted on-site, each one reflecting the unique terroir of the region.

For those with a curiosity about the winemaking process, a barrel room tasting offers a fascinating glimpse behind the scenes. Led by a knowledgeable member of the winemaking team, guests venture into the heart of the winery where oak barrels line the walls, housing wines in various stages of maturation. Using a specialized tool called a "wine thief," visitors can sample the evolving flavors straight from the barrel, gaining insight into the artistry of winemaking.

Meanwhile, a complete wine tour provides a comprehensive overview of the winery's operations, from vine to bottle. These tours often include visits to the vineyards, production facilities, barrel rooms, and tasting rooms, offering a holistic understanding of the winemaking process. Culminating in a delightful tasting session paired with gourmet cuisine, these tours are a feast for the senses.

Of course, no wine tasting journey would be complete without a visit to the wine bar. Here, guests can relax in a casual setting and sample a variety of wines, often served in flights for a comprehensive tasting experience. Paired with artisanal cheeses, meats, and small plates, the wine bar offers the perfect opportunity to savor the flavors of the region.

When it comes to choosing the right wine tasting experience for you and your companions, there are no hard and fast rules. Consider planning a wine tasting tour that encompasses a mix of experiences, allowing you to explore the diversity of the wine world and discover new favorites along the way. Whether you're drawn to the rustic charm of the vineyards or the sophistication of the tasting room, each stop on your journey promises to be a memorable one, filled with laughter, camaraderie, and of course, plenty of good wine.

# Girls' Trips and Misadventures: The Joy and Hilarity of Traveling With Your Chosen Sisters

Embarking on a girls' trip with your chosen sisters is more than just a vacation—it's an adventure filled with laughter, camaraderie, and unforgettable moments. From spontaneous dance parties in hotel rooms to navigating foreign cities with nothing but a sense of humor and a questionable map, traveling with your sisterhood promises a whirlwind of joy and hilarity.

In this exploration of girls' trips and misadventures, we delve into the experiences that make these journeys so special, celebrating the bonds of friendship forged through shared laughter and the unexpected twists and turns of travel. So grab your besties, pack your sense of adventure, and get ready to embark on a journey filled with laughter, mishaps, and memories that will last a lifetime.

Once upon a time, in the heart of a quaint little town nestled amidst the undulating vine-covered hills, there thrived a tight-knit group of friends who were bound together by their shared passion for adventure and their deep love for all things wine-related. Known affectionately throughout the town as the Wine Sisterhood, this eclectic group of kindred spirits had forged a bond that was as resilient as the vines that adorned the landscape.

Their journey into the world of wine began with a simple yet inspired idea: a girls' trip to explore the enchanting vineyards that dotted the countryside. As the first rays of dawn cast a golden glow upon the sleepy town, the Wine Sisterhood gathered around a weathered wooden table, their hearts aflutter with excitement and anticipation. Armed with maps, guidebooks, and an insatiable thirst for adventure, they eagerly delved into the delightful task of planning their epic wine-tasting escapade.

"Let us embark on this journey together," declared Emma, the group's resident wine aficionado, her eyes sparkling with excitement. "But first, we must research and plan meticulously." And so, they poured over maps of renowned wine regions, engaging in spirited discussions about their individual preferences and fervently jotting down notes on the must-visit wineries that peppered their route. From the robust reds of Bordeaux to the crisp whites of Burgundy, they dreamed of the exquisite wines they would taste and the unforgettable memories they would create.

Lily, the group's indefatigable organizer, chimed in with her own insights. "Accommodations are key to ensuring a comfortable and memorable experience," she declared, her fingers dancing across the keyboard as she scoured the internet for the perfect lodging options. With a palpable sense of excitement, they explored a myriad of possibilities, from charming bed and breakfasts nestled amidst sprawling vineyards to opulent villas boasting panoramic views of the rolling hills. Each accommodation was chosen with care, meticulously curated to complement their wine-tasting itinerary and provide a tranquil haven after a day of exploration and discovery.

As the planning continued, the Wine Sisterhood turned their attention to the logistics of transportation, a vital aspect of their upcoming adventure. "We must ensure that we have reliable and responsible transportation throughout our wine-tasting excursions," asserted Sarah, the group's pragmatic voice of reason. They debated the merits of designated drivers versus professional chauffeurs, weighing the pros and cons of each option before ultimately deciding to rotate the role among themselves, thereby ensuring that everyone had the opportunity to imbibe in the delightful wines without the burden of responsibility.

With their itinerary meticulously finalized and their accommodations secured, the Wine Sisterhood turned their attention to the practicalities of packing. "Let us not forget the essentials for wine tasting," admonished Mia, the group's level-headed pragmatist, as she began to assemble the necessary supplies. They carefully packed reusable wine glasses, a trusty corkscrew, and ample provisions of water to stay hydrated between tastings. And of course, they made sure to include an assortment of palate-cleansing snacks, for no wine-tasting adventure would be complete without a selection of delectable cheeses, crackers, and fruits to accompany the wines.

At long last, the day of their departure arrived, heralded by the soft hues of dawn breaking over the horizon. With hearts brimming with excitement and anticipation, the Wine Sisterhood set off on their grand adventure, their laughter mingling with the gentle rustle of the leaves and the sweet scent of grapes hanging heavy on the vine.

As they traversed the winding roads that led them from one vineyard to the next, the Wine Sisterhood immersed themselves in the rich tapestry of the local culture, engaging with vintners, winemakers, and tasting room staff to gain a deeper understanding of the region's winemaking traditions. They indulged in decadent food and wine pairings, savoring each exquisite flavor combination as they reveled in the joys of discovery and exploration.

Every moment of their journey was captured with meticulous care, as they snapped photos, recorded videos, and diligently documented their experiences in journals filled with colorful anecdotes and heartfelt reflections. From the sun-drenched vineyard vistas to the moonlit dinners spent under a canopy of stars, every detail was immortalized, a testament to the enduring bond of friendship that united them.

And as the sun dipped below the horizon on their final day of adventure, casting a warm glow over the landscape, the Wine Sisterhood gathered one last time to raise their glasses in a heartfelt toast to sisterhood, laughter, and the memories that would forever remain etched in their hearts. For in the end, it wasn't just about the wine—it was about the bonds they had forged, the laughter they had shared, and the extraordinary journey they had embarked upon together. Cheers to sisterhood, and to the endless possibilities that awaited on the next girls' trip!

# Cultural Cocktails and Conversations: Expanding Your Horizons, One Glass at a Time

In a world where the quest for cultural awareness is more important than ever, there lies an unconventional yet captivating pathway to expanding our horizons: through the rich history and diverse narratives of cocktails from around the globe. As we explore the origins of these beverages, we uncover not just the ingredients that make them but also the stories, traditions, and people behind them. This exploration can serve as a medium for deeper cultural understanding and personal growth, one glass at a time.

The journey into cultural cocktails is more than an adventure in taste; it's an immersive experience that connects us to different parts of the world. Take, for example, the Sangria of Spain, a refreshing concoction that has evolved over centuries. Originally, Sangria was a simple drink made by peasants from the leftover grapes they could not sell. Today, it symbolizes the Spanish zest for life, with its vibrant colors and fruity flavors, reminiscent of Spanish summers. This transformation from humble beginnings to a staple of Spanish culture speaks volumes about the country's history and its people's ability to create joy from simplicity.

Moving across the Atlantic, the Pisco Sour offers a glimpse into the heart of Peruvian identity. The debate over its origins with Chile adds a layer of intrigue, illustrating the complexities of cultural heritage and national pride. The cocktail's invention in the early 20th century by an American bartender in Lima showcases the fusion of local and foreign influences, a testament to Peru's rich cultural tapestry. Celebrating Pisco Sour Day, Peruvians pay homage not just to a drink but to their history and resilience.

In North America, the Sazerac tells the tale of New Orleans, a city with a vibrant mix of cultures. The evolution of the Sazerac from a cognac-based drink to one featuring rye whiskey mirrors the city's own transformation, influenced by waves of immigrants and changing times. Declared the official cocktail of New Orleans, the Sazerac is more than just a drink; it's a symbol of the city's enduring spirit and its blend of French, African, Spanish, and American cultures.

Crossing the pond to Britain, the story of the Pimm's No. 1 Cup reflects not just a beverage but a social tradition. From its origins as a health tonic to its status as a staple of British summertime, Pimm's embodies the British knack for conviviality and tradition. The drink's popularity at events like Wimbledon goes beyond its refreshing taste, symbolizing a collective cultural moment that unites people.

The Venetian Aperol Spritz offers a sip of Italian history, tracing back to the post-Napoleonic era. Its evolution from a simple wine spritzer to the iconic Aperol Spritz speaks to the Italian art of aperitivo, a cultural practice that brings people together to relax and socialize before dinner. The Aperol Spritz is not just a cocktail; it's an invitation to embrace the Italian way of life, where moments of togetherness are savored just like the drink itself.

Each of these cocktails—Sangria, Pisco Sour, Sazerac, Pimm's No. 1 Cup, and Aperol Spritz—carries within it stories of cultural fusion, adaptation, and identity. By delving into the origins and evolutions of these drinks, we engage in conversations that bridge cultures and expand our understanding of the world. This journey through cultural cocktails does not merely broaden our palate; it enriches our minds and souls, reminding us that every sip has a story, every flavor a heritage. So, the next time you raise a glass, remember that you're not just tasting a drink; you're savoring centuries of history, one glass at a time.

Remember, it's not just about the wine tasting around the world, from your living room to the vineyards of France; it's about the laughter that spills over the rim, the stories that flow more freely with every glass, and the unforgettable misadventures with your chosen sisters that become the stuff of legend.

In the spirit of expanding our horizons, one glass at a time, let's not forget the ultimate lesson learned from our adventures: that the best vintage is laughter, the finest aroma is joy, and the greatest taste is the sweetness of shared memories.

# CHAPTER 9

# Downward Dog and Dollars: Finding Financial Zen

Imagine your financial anxiety as a gremlin, not the cute, furry kind, but a sneaky creature that thrives on late fees and lost receipts. Now, picture yoga as the ancient, mystical warrior equipped with the serenity of a monk and the balance of a cat, ready to banish this pesky gremlin to the land of "I've-Got-This." Each sun salutation a step closer to financial zen, where due dates bow down to your newfound calm, and savings grow with the grace of a tree pose.

In the epic saga of your bank account, envision austerity and luxury as two dragons. One hoards your coins with a fiery glare, while the other tempts you toward treasure chests of fleeting pleasures. Your quest? To ride the middle dragon, the one that knows the value of a dollar but also when to soar through the skies for that metaphorical gourmet cheese that doesn't obliterate your wallet. It's the art of treating yourself without tipping the scales into the abyss of credit card despair.

Consider wealth not as a mountain of gold but as a garden where your well-being flowers under the sunshine of smart choices. Imagine investing in that yoga class as planting a seed that grows into a tree of tranquility, its leaves whispering secrets of balance and joy. Think of that home-cooked meal as watering the soil of contentment, where the fruits of health are more precious than the latest gadget.

In this delightful journey toward fiscal enlightenment, let the mantra be: harmony in finances, harmony in life. So yes, embrace that avocado, for in its green heart lies the gem of happiness, a testament to the fact that in the grand market of life, the best investments are those that nurture the soul.

# Yoga for Financial Anxiety:
# Breathing Through the Bills

In the sprawling metropolis of Mind and Body, there lies a quaint little district known as Financial Anxiety, where the residents often find themselves tangled in the vines of worry, their brows perpetually furrowed over the latest bill or the haunting specter of an empty savings account. It's a place where stress levels rise like skyscrapers, casting long shadows over the joy of daily life. But fear not, for there's a superhero in town, one whose powers transcend the conventional: Yoga, the ancient art of breathing through the bills.

Yoga, a beacon of tranquility in the bustling city of our minds, extends an invitation to explore the serene landscapes within us. It whispers of a magical formula where breath and movement intertwine to guide us toward a state of calm. This isn't about bending yourself into a pretzel or mastering the art of standing on your head while calculating your taxes. No, this is about meeting yourself where you are—amidst the chaos of unopened mail and due dates—and taking a few minutes each day to reconnect with your inner CFO, the Chief Feeling Officer.

Pranayama, the art of breath control, is the secret sauce in Yoga's toolkit. It's like having a direct line to calming the stormy seas of your mind. Through practices like the long exhale or diaphragmatic breathing, we can send a text message of peace to our brains, courtesy of the vagus nerve. This isn't just any message; it's the kind that gets VIP treatment, bypassing the clutter of daily thoughts and delivering a dose of calm directly to your nervous system.

But wait, before you jump into the Breath of Fire in hopes of burning away your financial worries, take heed. Not all breathwork is created equal in the realm of anxiety management. Some, like the invigorating *Kapalabhati*, are more like drinking a cup of espresso when what you really need is a soothing herbal tea. For the anxious mind, the steady rhythm of *Ujjayi* breathing, with its oceanic sound, can be the auditory lullaby that lulls your thoughts away from the cliff edge of worry.

Asanas, or yoga poses, serve as the scenic viewpoints along the journey, offering moments to pause and observe the landscape of our thoughts. These physical expressions are not just exercises in flexibility or strength; they are invitations to explore the present moment. Imagine transitioning into Warrior II, not as a battle against your financial woes but as a stance of strength and stability, facing the future with courage and grace.

In this practice, meditation becomes the ultimate destination, a place where the chatter of pending transactions and looming deadlines fades into the background. It's here, in the quiet meadow of mindfulness, that we learn to sit with our thoughts, observing them as they flutter by like leaves on a stream, without getting swept away in the current. This practice of self-regulation and awareness is akin to balancing your mental budget, ensuring that you're investing in thoughts that nurture peace and wellbeing.

So, how does one embark on this journey of fiscal serenity through yoga? Begin by carving out a small sanctuary in time and space, a few minutes each day where you can unroll your mat as you unroll your financial plans. Allow yourself to meet each worry with a breath, each doubt with a pose, and each moment of anxiety with mindfulness.

Remember, the path to financial enlightenment through yoga doesn't require you to renounce all worldly possessions or to master the most complex poses. It simply asks you to show up, breathe, and move with intention. In doing so, you'll find that the most significant investments aren't in stocks or bonds, but in the moments of connection between mind, body, and breath.

## Austerity Measures vs. Affordable Luxuries: Finding Balance in Your Budget

In the shimmering tableau of life's fiscal tightrope, single women are ingeniously scripting their saga, navigating the delicate dance between the thrift of austerity and the allure of affordable luxuries. It's akin to choosing between the virtuous simplicity of a kale salad and the sinful indulgence of a chocolate lava cake—a seemingly stark choice that, with a dash of creativity, transforms into an exquisite feast that satisfies both the palate and the purse.

Picture this: a universe where luxury doesn't equate to the price tag on a Birkin bag but is defined by the richness of experiences and the joy sparked by the things we truly love. It's a place where the concept of luxury is as personalized as your coffee order at that boutique café where the barista knows your life story.

Recall a moment when you indulged in something so sumptuous, so utterly divine, that the memory alone feels like a warm hug. Was it the item itself or the feeling it evoked? The truth is, luxury is the art of bathing in the golden rays of your own contentment, regardless of the bank balance. It's finding that sweet spot where pleasure meets prudence, allowing you to bask in the glow of financial wisdom without forgoing the champagne bubbles of life's delights.

For the fiercely independent woman, luxury might be an uninterrupted afternoon with a book in a bubble bath, rather than a weekend at a five-star spa. It's about transforming the mundane into the magnificent, one homemade facial at a time. It's the comfort of slipping into the world's softest pair of socks—yes, socks!—that didn't require maxing out a credit card but still feel like walking on clouds made of unicorn hair.

And let's talk about free time—the ultimate luxury in the age of the hustle. It's that elusive treasure we all yearn for, yet often squander like pennies in a wishing well. Imagine guarding your free time with the fierceness of a lioness protecting her cubs. Schedule it, cherish it, and for heaven's sake, don't feel guilty about basking in the sheer opulence of doing absolutely nothing. This, my friends, is the caviar of modern living.

Ah, but what of those irresistible whispers of lavishness that tug at our heartstrings? The siren call of that perfectly tailored dress that promises to morph you into a goddess? Fear not. The savvy woman knows that true style isn't bought but cultivated. It's hunting for treasures in thrift stores, swapping haute couture for haute craft, and understanding that the most powerful accessory is her confidence.

Quality over quantity is the mantra of the budget-conscious bon vivant. It's about investing in pieces that don't just fill the closet but enhance the soul. That one exquisite scarf that tells a story, or a pair of boots that have danced through life's ups and downs, are worth more than a mountain of fast fashion.

Dive into the DIY spa day with the zeal of a beauty guru on a mission. Light those candles, play your favorite tunes, and create a sanctuary where the stresses of the world melt away like the last remnants of a bath bomb. Luxury, after all, is about elevating the everyday into something extraordinary.

And for those moments when the digital world screams of others' jet-setting adventures, remember this: luxury is not a competition. It's not about matching the Instagram feeds of those who seem to live in a perpetual state of vacation. It's about crafting a life so rich in experiences and personal joys that the need for comparison evaporates like morning dew in the sunlight.

So, to all the fabulous single women out there navigating the balancing act between austerity measures and affordable luxuries, remember: your budget is not a constraint but a canvas. Paint it with the vibrant colors of your imagination, where every stroke is a testament to your ingenuity and flair for the art of living well. After all, the most luxurious life is one lived on your own terms, sparkling with the truest form of wealth—happiness.

## The Wealth of Well-Being: Prioritizing Health and Happiness Over Hoarding Pennies

In the bustling rhythm of modern life, single women often find themselves standing at the crossroads of financial prudence and emotional well-being, pondering whether to hoard pennies or invest in health and happiness. It's a nuanced dilemma that resonates deeply, reflecting the intricate dance between financial security and the pursuit of fulfillment.

Recent research has cast new light on this age-old question, revealing intriguing insights into the relationship between time, money, and happiness. Surveys conducted among over 1,000 graduating students from the University of British Columbia illuminated a fascinating trend: those who prioritized time over money tended to report higher levels of life satisfaction, even a year post-graduation. This suggests that while financial stability is undoubtedly important, the pursuit of wealth shouldn't overshadow the quest for joy and contentment (Dunn et al., 2020).

However, this isn't a call to abandon all financial responsibility. Wealth, in moderation, can indeed contribute to happiness, but its correlation with well-being isn't always straightforward. Surprisingly, studies suggest that the amount of money visible in our bank accounts can have a more significant impact on our happiness than our actual income level. This underscores the importance of managing finances wisely and finding a balance that allows for both financial security and emotional fulfillment.

So, how can single women navigate this delicate balance between financial prudence and personal happiness? The answer lies in embracing mindful spending habits and prioritizing experiences over material possessions. Research consistently shows that people derive more joy and satisfaction from memorable experiences like travel, concerts, and meaningful interactions than from the accumulation of material goods. By focusing on creating cherished memories and nurturing meaningful connections, single women can cultivate a sense of fulfillment that transcends the limitations of material wealth.

Moreover, investing in time-saving measures can be a powerful way to enhance overall well-being. In today's fast-paced world, where time is a precious commodity, outsourcing tasks and responsibilities can free up valuable time for self-care, relaxation, and pursuing activities that bring joy and fulfillment. Whether it's hiring a cleaning service, outsourcing errands, or simply carving out moments for rest and relaxation, investing in time-saving measures can have a profound impact on mental and emotional well-being.

Additionally, acts of generosity and giving back to others can be a potent source of happiness and fulfillment. Research has shown that helping others and engaging in acts of kindness can boost mood, reduce stress, and foster a sense of connection and purpose. Whether it's volunteering, making charitable donations, or simply offering a helping hand to those in need, acts of generosity can enrich our lives and contribute to a greater sense of happiness and fulfillment.

In the grand tapestry of life, each expenditure becomes a stroke, painting a portrait of our values, priorities, and aspirations. By embracing mindful spending habits, prioritizing experiences over material possessions, investing in time-saving measures, and giving back to others, single women can create lives that are rich in meaning, purpose, and fulfillment. In doing so, they can find a delicate balance between financial prudence and personal happiness, ensuring that every penny spent contributes to a life well-lived.

To all the fabulous single women out there navigating the twists and turns of financial responsibility and personal well-being, remember this: in the grand adventure of life, balance is the ultimate treasure map. Whether you're striking a pose in yoga class, indulging in affordable luxuries, or prioritizing your health and happiness, know that every breath, every budget decision, and every moment of self-care is a step toward a richer, more fulfilling life. So, breathe through the bills, find harmony in your financial journey, and embrace the wealth of well-being that awaits. After all, in the grand saga of "Austerity Measures vs. Affordable Luxuries," you're the leading lady—and your happiness is the ultimate plot twist!

# CHAPTER 10

# The Single Woman's Culinary Adventures

Welcome to the delightful world of cooking for one, where every meal is a rendezvous with yourself, and you're both the master chef and the enchanted diner. Picture this: you, adorned in an apron and wielding a spatula like a knight with his sword, bravely facing the kitchen battlefield. Burnt toast? Ah, just a touch of charred elegance. Overly spicy chili? A fiery dance on your taste buds. Embrace the mishaps, for they are the spices of life in this culinary escapade.

But who says solo dining can't be a gourmet affair? Bid farewell to bland microwave dinners as you elevate them to epicurean heights. Pair that frozen lasagna with a velvety Chianti, or let a playful Pinot Grigio flirt with your mac 'n' cheese. It's not just about what's on your plate; it's about the symphony of flavors you orchestrate around it, turning the mundane into the extraordinary.

And what of leftovers? Fear not, for they are not relics of overindulgence but rather canvases for your culinary creativity. That lone serving of pasta? It's the star ingredient in tomorrow's frittata or a midnight snack masterpiece. Leftovers are not burdens but challenges, puzzles waiting to be solved with a dash of ingenuity and a sprinkle of spice.

So, dear lady, join us on this gastronomic odyssey, where every meal is an adventure, every mishap a lesson, and every bite a celebration of the joy of cooking for one. Prepare to dazzle your palate, astonish your senses, and fall in love with the most delightful company of all—yourself.

# Cooking for One: A Love Affair: Discovering the Joy of Cooking (and Eating) Alone

In the bustling kitchen of life, there's a corner that often goes unnoticed—a cozy nook where pots and pans sing solo ballads, where spatulas perform daring solos, and where the only critic is the gentle sizzle of ingredients in the pan. Welcome to the enchanting world of cooking for one.

Cooking and eating for one is often painted as a lonely endeavor, a wasteful voyage into the depths of the kitchen, armed with pots and pans and little else. But let me tell you, dear reader, it's a journey worth embarking on—a delightful dance of flavors, textures, and culinary discoveries.

While the idea of cooking for oneself may seem daunting at first glance, it's a rewarding experience that holds untold treasures. It's about more than just feeding your body—it's about nourishing your soul with wholesome, homemade goodness. And trust me, there's nothing quite like the satisfaction of savoring a meal crafted with your own two hands.

Contrary to popular belief, cooking for one isn't a chore—it's a canvas for creativity. When you're the sole chef in your kitchen domain, you wield the spatula like a paintbrush, creating culinary masterpieces tailored to your unique tastes. Love garlic? Pile it on! Can't stand cilantro? Banish it from your culinary kingdom! The beauty of cooking for one lies in the freedom to experiment, to explore, and to indulge without reservation.

But ah, the art of portion control—how to navigate the sea of servings when dining alone? Fear not, for in the world of solo cooking, you hold the power. No more oversized portions or wasted leftovers languishing in the fridge. When you're the sole diner, you have the liberty to craft perfectly portioned meals, each bite a harmonious symphony of flavor and nutrition.

And let's not forget the joy of culinary experimentation! Cooking for one is your ticket to culinary creativity, a playground where you can unleash your inner chef without the pressure of pleasing others. From sushi-making adventures to sauce-simmering escapades, the kitchen is your oyster, and the possibilities are endless.

But wait, there's more! In the realm of solo cooking, time-saving hacks reign supreme. Meal prepping, kitchen gadgets, and easy-to-follow recipes become your trusted allies in the battle against hunger and monotony. With a little planning and a sprinkle of ingenuity, you can whip up delicious meals in no time, leaving you more time to savor the fruits of your labor.

Ah, but what about the siren call of takeout and prepackaged meals? While tempting, they pale in comparison to the joys of home-cooked goodness. That's where meal planning comes into play—a simple yet powerful strategy for ensuring you always have delicious and nutritious meals at your fingertips.

Meal planning is not just a practical necessity; it's an art form—a delicate dance of flavors, textures, and culinary dreams. Picture yourself, armed with a pen and paper, mapping out your culinary adventures for the week ahead. Breakfast burritos on Monday, stir-fry on Tuesday, and perhaps a hearty soup on Wednesday—the possibilities are as endless as your imagination.

But meal planning isn't just about ensuring you have something to eat—it's about nourishing your body and soul with wholesome, homemade goodness. By taking the time to plan your meals and snacks, you're not only ensuring you're eating well but also savoring the joy of anticipation—a delicious reward waiting at the end of each day.

And let's not forget the thrill of the grocery store—a treasure trove of ingredients just waiting to be transformed into culinary delights. Armed with your shopping list and a sense of culinary adventure, you navigate the aisles with the finesse of a seasoned chef, selecting the freshest produce, the finest cuts of meat, and the most tantalizing spices.

But perhaps the greatest joy of cooking for one lies in the act itself—

the rhythmic chopping of vegetables, the gentle sizzle of onions in the pan, the intoxicating aroma of garlic and herbs wafting through the air. In these moments, you are not just a cook—you are an artist, creating a masterpiece one ingredient at a time.

So, my fellow culinary adventurers, fear not the journey into Cooking for One: A Love Affair. Embrace the solitude of the kitchen, wield your spatula like a sword, and let your taste buds be your guide. For in the world of solo cooking, every meal is a celebration of self-indulgence, every bite a testament to the joy of culinary discovery. So grab your apron, sharpen your knives, and let the adventure begin!

## Wine Pairings for Microwave Dinners: Elevating Your Solo Dining Experience

In the grand symphony of culinary delights, few things elevate the solo dining experience quite like a perfectly paired glass of wine. Whether you're indulging in a quick microwave dinner or whipping up a gourmet feast for one, the right wine can transform your meal from ordinary to extraordinary, tantalizing your taste buds and enhancing your culinary adventure.

When it comes to pairing wine with microwave dinners, it's essential to consider the primary elements of both the dish and the wine. By understanding how these elements interact, you can create harmonious flavor combinations that elevate your solo dining experience to new heights.

Let's delve into the six primary elements of wine and food pairings and explore some delightful combinations that will take your microwave dinners from mundane to magnificent.

1.  **Fat:** Microwave dinners often contain varying levels of fat, which can present an exciting opportunity for wine pairing. Wines with high acidity or robust tannins can help balance the richness of fatty foods, creating a harmonious dining experience. Pairing suggestion: Indulge in a juicy microwave burger with a glass of

Cabernet Sauvignon. The wine's fruit flavors and robust tannins will complement the meaty richness of the burger, elevating your solo dining experience to new heights.

2.  **Salt:** Salt can be a challenging element to pair with wine, as it can strip the fruit notes from certain wines and make them taste bitter. However, wines with high acidity can help balance the saltiness of dishes, creating a delightful contrast of flavors. Pairing suggestion: Enjoy a microwave meal of briny shrimp scampi with a crisp Sauvignon Blanc. The wine's bright acidity will cleanse your palate and accentuate the rich flavors of the shrimp, creating a memorable dining experience.

3.  **Acid/Sour:** Acidic foods pair beautifully with wines that share similar acidity levels. By matching the acidity of the dish with the acidity of the wine, you can create a harmonious flavor profile that enhances the overall dining experience. Pairing suggestion: Savor a microwave chicken piccata with a glass of Chardonnay. The wine's citrusy notes and crisp acidity will complement the tangy flavors of the lemon sauce, creating a deliciously balanced pairing.

4.  **Sweet:** When pairing wine with sweet dishes, it's essential to ensure that the wine is sweeter than the dessert to avoid a tart or bitter taste. Look for wines with varying degrees of sweetness to find the perfect match for your microwave dinner. Pairing suggestion: Indulge in a decadent microwave chocolate lava cake with a glass of Ruby Port. The wine's sweet, fruity flavors will complement the rich chocolatey goodness of the cake, creating a delightful finale to your solo dining experience.

5.  **Bitter:** Bitterness in food can be challenging to pair with wine, as it can intensify the bitterness of certain wines and create an unpleasant taste. However, wines with fruity or earthy notes can help balance the bitterness of the dish, creating a harmonious flavor combination. Pairing suggestion: Delight in a microwave roasted vegetable medley with a glass of Pinot Noir. The wine's earthy undertones and fruity flavors will complement the roasted vegetables, creating a satisfying and flavorful pairing.

6.  **Texture/Umami:** Foods with rich textures or umami flavors pair beautifully with wines that share similar characteristics. Look for wines with bold flavors and robust tannins to complement the hearty flavors of your microwave dinner. Pairing suggestion: Savor a microwave lasagna with a glass of Malbec. The wine's bold fruit flavors and silky texture will complement the layers of pasta, cheese, and sauce, creating a luxurious and indulgent pairing.

In conclusion, while microwave dinners may seem like a humble meal choice, with the right wine pairing, they can become a culinary adventure worthy of celebration. By considering the primary elements of both the dish and the wine, you can create harmonious flavor combinations that elevate your solo dining experience to new heights. So raise a glass, savor each bite, and toast to the joy of microwave dinners paired with the perfect wine. Cheers!

## "I Made Too Much Pasta Again": Embracing the Leftovers Lifestyle

In the bustling city of New York, where time is a luxury and kitchen space comes at a premium, Glenda (our person of choice who will aid our understanding) found herself navigating the solo dining scene with gusto. With a busy schedule and a penchant for efficiency, she quickly realized the potential of leftovers to revolutionize her culinary routine. Here are some of Glenda's tried and tested tips for making the most of leftovers and minimizing waste in the solo kitchen:

1.  **Meal Planning With Leftovers:** Glenda understood the power of meal planning, and leftovers were a crucial component of her strategy. By intentionally cooking larger portions, she ensured that she had ample leftovers to enjoy throughout the week. From hearty stews to flavorful curries, Glenda embraced the leftovers lifestyle with enthusiasm, knowing that each meal saved her precious time and effort.

2.  **Repurposing Leftovers:** Leftover proteins and veggies were never wasted in Glenda's kitchen. Instead, she transformed them

into delicious new creations that rivaled the original dishes. From tacos and burritos to soups and salads, Glenda's culinary creativity knew no bounds. By repurposing leftovers, she not only minimized waste but also enjoyed a diverse array of flavors and textures in her meals.

3. **Organizing the Freezer**: Glenda's freezer was a well-organized treasure trove of culinary delights. She utilized ziplock bags to portion and store raw meat, fish, and chopped vegetables, maximizing space and minimizing waste. By allocating different sections of her freezer to various food categories and rotating items regularly, Glenda ensured that nothing went to waste.

4. **Maximizing Fresh Produce**: Fresh produce was a precious commodity in Glenda's kitchen, and she took great care to make it last. By cleaning and lining her vegetable drawer with kitchen roll, she prevented excess condensation and prolonged the lifespan of her veggies. Glenda also repurposed plastic trays from the supermarket to keep her vegetable drawer tidy and organized.

5. **Getting Creative with Preservation**: Glenda wasn't afraid to get creative when it came to preserving produce. Whether it was canning surplus fruits and vegetables or baking with overripe bananas, she found inventive ways to reduce waste and extend the life of her groceries. By embracing preservation techniques, Glenda enjoyed the fruits of her labor long after they were harvested.

6. **Knowing When to "Use By"**: While Glenda was mindful of use-by dates, she also knew that they weren't always set in stone. With a keen sense of food safety and an understanding of which foods could be safely consumed past their use-by dates, she avoided unnecessary waste and made the most of every ingredient in her kitchen.

7. **Customizing Storage Space**: Glenda tailored her food storage space to suit her lifestyle and kitchen layout. Whether it was using jars to store dry goods, wrapping apples in newspaper to

extend their shelf life, or utilizing every nook and cranny of her pantry, she optimized her storage space to minimize waste and maximize efficiency.

In the bustling metropolis of New York City, Glenda had mastered the art of solo dining through her innovative approach to leftovers and food storage. With a few simple strategies and a dash of creativity, she transformed mundane meals into culinary delights, all while reducing waste and saving time in the kitchen. As Glenda liked to say, "Embracing the leftovers lifestyle isn't just about minimizing waste—it's about maximizing flavor and enjoying every bite along the way."

As we bid adieu to our culinary adventures in the realm of solo dining, let us raise a toast to the joy of cooking (and eating) alone. From exploring the intricate dance of wine pairings for microwave dinners to embracing the leftovers lifestyle with a hearty "I Made Too Much Pasta Again," we've embarked on a gastronomic journey filled with laughter, creativity, and perhaps a few burnt toast mishaps along the way.

But through it all, we've discovered the true essence of dining solo—it's not just about feeding ourselves, but about nourishing our souls with the warmth of homemade meals, the delight of a well-paired wine, and the satisfaction of turning leftovers into culinary masterpieces.

So whether you find yourself savoring a gourmet microwave dinner paired with a robust Chianti or delighting in the creative repurposing of last night's pasta into a frittata fit for a king, remember this: cooking for one is not just a necessity, but a love affair—a joyful celebration of self-reliance, resourcefulness, and the simple pleasure of a delicious meal enjoyed in the company of none other than yourself.

Here's to the joy of cooking for one—a love affair that knows no bounds and brings endless delight to the solo diner's table. Cheers to culinary adventures, flavorful discoveries, and the undeniable magic of a well-prepared meal enjoyed in solitude. As we continue to explore the culinary wonders of solo dining, may our hearts be full, our glasses never empty, and our kitchens forever bustling with the delicious aroma of possibility.

# CHAPTER 11

# The Literary Guide to Love and Loneliness

Welcome to the wild and wondrous world of love, literature, and life lessons—a place where romance novels set our hearts aflutter, poetry offers solace sweeter than a tub of ice cream, and biographies of badass women make us want to conquer the world solo.

Imagine a realm where every encounter isn't just a chance meeting but a prelude to a steamy romance, where every protagonist isn't just rugged but possesses abs that could grate cheese. Ah, yes, the world of romance novels—where reality takes a backseat and fantasy reigns supreme. But let's face it, expecting life to mirror these tales is like expecting your toaster to recite Shakespeare at breakfast. Utterly delightful, yet profoundly improbable.

So, when life hands you lemons (or questionable love interests), why not turn to the soothing embrace of poetry? Because, my friends, in the realm of rhymes, even heartbreak can be spun into something resembling art—minus the extra calories of comfort food. Poetry teaches us that pain is but a passing cloud, and with a sprinkle of creativity, it can transform into a rainbow of emotions, or at least a mildly coherent verse.

And let us not forget the tales of fierce, fabulous females whose biographies read like roadmaps through the wilderness of singledom. From Amelia Earhart's solo flights to Frida Kahlo's brushstrokes of brilliance, these women show us that the path to greatness need not be paved with rose petals and romance. No, sometimes it's the journey of self-discovery, the pursuit of passion, and the unyielding spirit within that lead us to our own version of happily ever after.

So, my fellow adventurers in the bookish realm, let us embark on this literary escapade together, armed with humor, heart, and perhaps a healthy dose of skepticism. For in the pages of romance, poetry, and biography, we find not just stories, but echoes of our own triumphs, tribulations, and the ever-present reminder that life is far too extraordinary to be confined to the pages of a novel.

## Romance Novels vs. Reality: Learning From Fiction Without Expecting a Fairytale

In the unpredictable journey of life, where paths twist and tales unfold in an unscripted manner, romance novels stand as the cherished interlude we all crave—a realm infused with dreams, desires, and the intoxicating allure of love. Yet, as we turn each page, drenched in the desire and drama of our favorite characters, a curious question lingers: can the lessons of fiction guide us through the reality of romance without leading us astray in search of a fairytale? Let's dive into this delightful conundrum, shall we?

Romance novels, bless their hearts, paint a world where every hero, no matter how brooding, has a core of gold ripe for discovery, and every heroine is a beacon of strength, wit, and unfailing resilience. In these tales, women are not merely characters; they are powerhouses of potential, embodying every dream from princess to epidemiologist, from sword-wielding warriors to astrophysicists. And the men? Oh, they are the epitome of respect, love, and kindness—a rare breed that might leave you scouring your local coffee shops with a sense of hopeful desperation.

But here lies the rub: expecting life to mimic these novels is akin to waiting for a pumpkin carriage at the stroke of midnight. Amusing? Absolutely. Likely? Not so much.

Real relationships, unlike their fictional counterparts, are beautifully messy tapestries woven from moments of misunderstanding, growth, and compromise. They lack the predictability of a romance novel's guaranteed happy ending, instead offering a rollercoaster ride of emotions and experiences that, while often challenging, are incredibly rewarding.

Ah, conflict. In romance novels, it's the delicious tension that keeps us flipping pages into the wee hours of the morning—the misunderstanding that could be solved with a single conversation, yet somehow spirals into a saga. These moments are not just about the drama; they offer a canvas to explore the resolution, showcasing communication, trust, and commitment as the heroes of the day.

In the real world, however, conflicts are less about stolen kisses in the rain and more about who forgot to buy milk—again. The beauty? It's in these mundane moments that the true essence of a healthy relationship shines, teaching us that love is not just about grand gestures but the small, daily acts of kindness and understanding.

Romance novels are a testament to the boundless potential of women, featuring heroines who are as diverse in their ambitions as they are unified in their strength. They remind us that we, too, can be anything we dream of, from billionaires to single parents, thriving against all odds.

Yet, it's crucial to remember that while fiction offers inspiration, our real-life stories are equally deserving of celebration. We may not all wield swords or solve complex equations by day's end, but our daily victories—in personal growth, in kindness, in surviving and thriving—are no less significant.

So, how do we navigate the enchanting world of romance novels without losing sight of reality? The key lies in embracing these stories for what they are: beautiful escapades into the realm of what could be, sprinkled with lessons that can indeed enrich our real-world relationships.

· **Appreciate the Fantasy, Live the Reality**: Let the courage, resilience, and adventurous spirit of your favorite characters inspire you, but remember to cherish the beauty in life's imperfections and the unique journey of your own relationship.

· **Seek the Core, Not the Caricature**: Emulate the qualities of respect, love, and kindness found in idealized characters, but seek them in the beautifully flawed human beings around us, knowing that perfection is a myth both in love and in life.

· **Celebrate Your Story**: Remember that your life, with its ups, downs, and everything in between, is as epic a tale as any penned by the most imaginative authors. You are the protagonist of your own story—make it one worth reading.

In the end, romance novels offer a window into a world where love conquers all, and dreams are just a page turn away. Yet, it's in the unscripted chaos of reality that we find the true depth of love, learning, and life. Here's to finding inspiration in fiction without losing the wonder of our own beautifully imperfect love stories.

## Poetry for the Pain: Finding Solace in Sonnets and Haikus

In the vast canvas of existence, where emotions ebb and flow like the tides of the sea, poetry emerges as both a sanctuary and a guide—a luminous beacon illuminating the path through the labyrinth of life's trials and tribulations. Within the delicate cadence of verse, we discover not only solace for our weary souls but also the transformative power to shape our own narratives, to express the depths of our emotions, and to navigate the tumultuous waters of existence with grace and resilience.

Consider for a moment the myriad ways in which poetry serves as a lifeline in our darkest hours. In Emily Dickinson's timeless masterpiece, *Hope is the Thing with Feathers*, we find not merely words on a page but a melody of resilience—a whispered promise that even in the depths of despair, hope remains an unwavering presence, a steadfast companion guiding us through the storm. Here, in the delicate flutter of a bird's wing, we find solace in the knowledge that even the smallest glimmer of hope can illuminate the darkest of nights.

And what of reconciliation, that delicate dance between estranged hearts yearning to find their way back to one another? In Rumi's ethereal poem, *Out Beyond Ideas*, we encounter not only a call to forgiveness but also a roadmap to healing—a gentle reminder that true reconciliation lies not in the realm of the intellect but in the boundless expanse of the heart. Here, amidst the vastness of the universe, we discover the transformative power of love—the unbreakable bond that transcends differences and unites us in our shared humanity.

But poetry is not merely a vessel for the wisdom of ages past—it is also a medium through which we can explore and express our own deepest emotions, forging connections with others and finding solace in shared experiences. Indeed, the act of writing poetry can be a profoundly cathartic experience, allowing us to channel our pain, our joy, and our hopes into words that resonate with the very essence of our being.

So, how does one begin to write their own poetry, you may ask? Fear not, dear reader, for the process need not be daunting. Begin by immersing yourself in the works of poets both past and present, allowing their words to inspire and guide you on your own poetic journey. Take note of the techniques they employ, the imagery they evoke, and the emotions they convey, and allow yourself to be swept away by the beauty of language.

Next, find a quiet space where you can reflect and let your thoughts flow freely. Perhaps it is a sunlit corner of your favorite café or a secluded spot in nature where you feel most at peace. Close your eyes, take a deep breath, and allow your mind to wander—to the deepest recesses of your soul, where the rawest emotions lie waiting to be expressed.

And finally, put pen to paper (or fingers to keyboard) and let the words pour forth like water from a spring, uninhibited and unfiltered. Do not worry about structure or form at first—simply allow yourself to write freely, letting your thoughts and feelings guide the way. Remember, poetry is not about perfection but about authenticity, about capturing the essence of who you are and what you feel in that moment.

As you continue to write and explore, you may find yourself drawn to certain themes or subjects—love, loss, nature, spirituality—whatever speaks to your heart. Embrace these themes wholeheartedly, allowing them to shape and inform your poetry in ways both profound and unexpected.

And above all, do not be afraid to share your work with others. Whether it's with a trusted friend, a supportive community, or the wider world, sharing your poetry can be a deeply rewarding experience, opening up new avenues for connection, understanding, and growth.

In the end, remember that poetry is not just a form of expression but a journey—a journey of self-discovery, of exploration, and of transformation. So, dear reader, take up your pen and embark on this wondrous adventure, for in the words of Langston Hughes, "Hold fast to dreams, for if dreams die, life is a broken-winged bird that cannot fly."

## Biographies as Beacons: Drawing Strength From the Stories of Strong, Single Women Before Us

In the sweeping expanse of human history, where tales of triumph and turmoil mingle like characters at a grand ball, biographies stand as beacons of inspiration—illuminating the paths trodden by the fearless, the fierce, and the fabulously single. For in the stories of strong women who came before us, we find not only echoes of our own struggles and triumphs but also a roadmap to resilience, empowerment, and unapologetic self-discovery.

Biographies and memoirs, dear reader, are not mere collections of facts and figures but vibrant tapestries woven from the threads of human experience. They serve as portals to the past, offering glimpses into lives lived boldly, passionately, and unapologetically. From the dusty pages of history emerge the voices of trailblazers, pioneers, and visionaries—women who dared to defy convention, challenge the status quo, and carve out their own destinies in a world determined to silence them.

Consider, if you will, the remarkable story of Pauli Murray—a firebrand activist whose pen was as mighty as any sword. In *The Firebrand and the First Lady* by Patricia Bell-Scott, we are introduced to a woman whose name may have faded from the annals of history, but whose legacy looms large in the fight for civil rights. From her groundbreaking correspondence with Eleanor Roosevelt to her tireless advocacy for racial and gender equality, Murray's story serves as a reminder that even the smallest voices can spark monumental change.

And then there is Sonya Sotomayor, the trailblazing jurist whose ascent to the highest court in the land is nothing short of awe-inspiring. In *My Beloved World*, Sotomayor invites us into the inner sanctum of her life, sharing the trials and triumphs that shaped her into the formidable force she is today. From her humble beginnings in a tumultuous household to her historic appointment to the Supreme Court, Sotomayor's journey is a testament to the power of perseverance, passion, and unwavering determination.

But it is not only the well-known figures of history who deserve our attention—it is also the unsung heroes whose contributions have long been overlooked and underestimated. Take, for example, Pamela Colman Smith—a name perhaps unfamiliar to many, yet whose artistic legacy has left an indelible mark on the world of tarot. In *Pamela Colman Smith: The Untold Story*, authors Stuart Kaplan, Elizabeth Foley O'Connor, Malinda Boyd Parsons, and Mary K Greer shed light on the life and work of this extraordinary woman, whose illustrations continue to captivate and inspire to this day. From her early days in the UK to her later years in Jamaica and America, Colman Smith's journey is a testament to the power of creativity, resilience, and unbridled passion.

But perhaps the most remarkable aspect of these biographies is not merely the stories they tell, but the lessons they impart—the reminders that we, too, possess the strength, the courage, and the resilience to overcome any obstacle that stands in our way. For in the tales of strong, single women who came before us, we find not only mirrors of our own potential but also guides to unlocking the boundless possibilities that lie within each and every one of us.

So, dear reader, let us raise our metaphorical glasses to the women who paved the way, who shattered glass ceilings, and who dared to dream of a world where anything is possible. And let us draw strength from their stories, their struggles, and their triumphs— for in their footsteps, we find the courage to forge our own paths, to write our own stories, and to embrace the fierce, fabulous, and fearlessly single women we were always meant to be. Cheers to that!

And remember, folks, while romance novels may promise us a knight in shining armor, poetry may offer solace for our soul, and biographies may illuminate the paths of the fearless, the most important lesson of all is this: in the game of love and life, it's okay to occasionally trade the sword for a feather duster and the fairytale ending for a good laugh and a tub of ice cream. After all, who needs a prince when you've got a pint of Ben & Jerry's and a Netflix queue full of rom-coms? Cheers to embracing the imperfections of reality and finding the humor in every happily ever after!

# CHAPTER 12

# Crafting Your Own Happy Endings

Step into your own spotlight, because who says you need a crowd to celebrate? From conquering the latest project at work to nailing that elusive French braid, every personal victory deserves its moment in the sun. So, pop that champagne bottle for one and revel in the glory of acing life's little tests. Solo celebrations aren't just about patting yourself on the back; they're a declaration of self-love, a nod to your accomplishments without seeking external validation. After all, the most important approval comes from within—perhaps with a side glance from your feline friend, if you're lucky.

Your home is more than just four walls; it's your sanctuary, a canvas for your quirks, dreams, and the remarkable journey you're on. Forget the glossy pages of 'perfect' home decor magazines; your space should echo your story, from the concert tickets adorning the fridge to the mismatched mugs that tell tales of adventures past. Decorating becomes a form of self-expression, turning your living space into a visual diary of life's most vibrant moments. Hang that painting you adore, even if it's just because it complements the sofa, and surround yourself with objects that make your heart dance with joy every time you cross the threshold.

The future looms ahead, a vast expanse of uncertainty and "what ifs." Yet, rather than seeing it as a daunting challenge, embrace this uncertainty with open arms, for it holds the promise of endless possibilities. Raise a glass of fine wine, each sip a tribute to the adventures yet to unfold. Crafting your own happy ending isn't about erasing uncertainty but rather embracing it as part of the journey. Whether your story is one of solo triumphs or chapters filled with love and laughter from your chosen family, remember this: the best narratives are the ones where the protagonist—yes, that's you—believes in the enchantment of their own tale.

## The Art of Solo Celebrations: Making Every Achievement a Reason to Celebrate

In a world that often seems to rush past us, pausing to celebrate our personal achievements is a vital act of self-love and acknowledgment. It's a recognition that our journey, with its unique ups and downs, is worth celebrating. Making every achievement a reason to celebrate transforms our relationship with ourselves and our aspirations, turning life into a series of moments worth savoring.

Firstly, understanding that celebrating oneself doesn't necessitate an audience is crucial. It's a deeply personal journey where the act of celebration is as unique as the individual. Whether it's indulging in your favorite meal, embarking on a solo journey to uncharted destinations, or simply dancing away in the solitude of your living room, the essence of celebration is about honoring your worth and achievements. The method of celebration should be a reflection of your personality, desires, and joys. From a tranquil spa day to a thrilling adventure or a serene evening at home, the manner of celebration should resonate with your soul. The key is to unapologetically embrace your method of celebration, free from the constraints and expectations of others.

Celebrating our achievements injects us with a vital dose of enthusiasm. This enthusiasm acts as a rejuvenating force, fueling our passion and empowering us to tackle future challenges with renewed vigor. It closes the loop of effort and reward, making the journey toward our goals as rewarding as the achievement itself. Enthusiasm is the lifeblood of all great endeavors, nurturing the passion required to pursue excellence.

Moreover, celebrating our successes plays a pivotal role in building confidence. This confidence is twofold. On one hand, it cultivates an inner belief in our abilities, reassuring us that the achievements we've secured are stepping stones to even greater accomplishments. On the other, it fosters the trust and belief others place in us. Achievements not only elevate our self-esteem but also signal to the world our capability and reliability, opening doors to new opportunities and fruitful relationships.

The importance of consistently celebrating achievements cannot be overstated. It's not merely about acknowledging the end result but also about valuing the dedication, resilience, and energy we've poured into our endeavors. This consistency in applying ourselves, maintaining focus, and harnessing our passion is what breeds success. Celebrating this repeated effort and mindset reinforces our commitment to our goals and is a testament to our perseverance.

Embracing the thrill of achievement fosters a unique kind of audacity within us. It's that sly smirk of self-assurance, that whisper of boldness urging us to dream bigger and dare more. This sensation is a powerful motivator, nudging us toward contemplating what other heights we might scale. It's the realization that perhaps we possess the right mix of madness and method to pursue even bolder visions.

In celebrating every achievement, we do more than just mark milestones; we weave a rich tapestry of memorable moments that highlight our journey's significance. Each celebration is a note to ourselves, reminding us of our capability, resilience, and the beauty of our aspirations. It's about turning our life's narrative into one that vibrates with joy, achievements, and continuous growth.

Moreover, these celebrations are acts of mindfulness, enabling us to live in the present and appreciate the fruits of our labor. They remind us that while aspirations drive us forward, it's the journey and its achievements, both big and small, that enrich our lives. By making every achievement a reason to celebrate, we not only honor our efforts but also create a reservoir of positive energy and motivation that propels us forward.

In essence, celebrating our achievements is a celebration of ourselves, our journey, and the endless possibilities that lie ahead. It's a declaration that we are on a path of continuous growth, learning, and joy. So, let's raise a glass to our achievements, to the resilience and passion that got us here, and to the thrilling prospects that await. Because in the grand narrative of our lives, every achievement, no matter how small, is a chapter worth celebrating.

## Building a Home That Reflects You: Decorating Your Space as a Sanctuary for Your Soul

Ah, the art of crafting a sanctuary—not just any room, but a soulful retreat that speaks to the very essence of tranquility and inner peace. This endeavor, my dear reader, is akin to embarking on a mystical quest for the Holy Grail, but fear not! For I shall be your guide, leading you through enchanted forests of decor and over the serene waters of ambiance to create a haven that is a sanctuary for your soul. Let's begin this magical journey, shall we?

The first step in our quest involves summoning the right atmosphere through the alchemy of color and light. Imagine painting with all the hues of the wind—cool blues and gentle greens that whisper the ancient secrets of calm and peace. These aren't just colors; they are the soul's comfort food, nourishing and soothing with every glance.

Light, the ever-faithful companion of color, plays its part by casting spells of warmth and coziness. Imagine the soft glow of dawn that greets you with a gentle hug, or the tender embrace of dusk, wrapping you in layers of comfort. This is the power of carefully chosen ambient lighting, with candles flickering like tiny fireflies, guiding you back to your inner peace.

Our next chapter in this saga leads us to the realm of furniture—a kingdom where comfort and style reign supreme. Here, we seek the legendary seating that promises endless comfort without sacrificing an iota of elegance. Picture a throne of plush cushions that cradles you after a long day's quest, or a chaise that whispers tales of old-world charm and modern-day chic. In this kingdom, every piece is a loyal subject to your kingdom of relaxation, marrying function with flair in a harmonious union.

As we journey further, we encounter the treasures of decoration, each piece a gem imbued with the power to transform and uplift. This realm is rich with serene landscapes painted in soothing hues, sculptures that tell tales of tranquility, and artisanal crafts that carry the essence of peace. These aren't mere objects; they're your allies, each contributing to the sanctuary's soul with its unique story and aura.

No quest for sanctuary is complete without paying homage to our eternal ally—Mother Nature. By inviting the outdoors in, we cultivate a bond with the earth that grounds and nourishes our spirit. Indoor foliage becomes our green guardians, purifying the air and connecting us to the web of life. The gentle murmur of a water feature becomes our sanctuary's heartbeat, reminding us of the ebb and flow of existence. In this space, every natural element is a piece of the puzzle, completing the picture of your soulful retreat.

As we near the end of our quest, we discover the enchanting world of aromatherapy, where scents wield the power to transport and transform. Here, lavender is not just a plant, but a potion for relaxation, and sandalwood a charm against the chaos of the world. This magical practice invites you to blend and brew your own concoctions, creating a signature scent that is a beacon of peace for your soul.

The final enchantment in our journey is the infusion of personal touches—those unique elements that make the space unmistakably yours. Whether it's a collection of cherished books, a tapestry of woven memories, or an altar of personal relics, these touches are the final spell that binds the sanctuary to your spirit. They remind you that this is not just any retreat, but your personal haven, a sacred space where your soul is free to soar.

And so, our quest comes to a close, with each step along the path weaving together to create a sanctuary that is a testament to your unique journey. This haven, forged from the magic of color, light, nature, and personal touches, stands as a sanctuary not just for your soul, but as a sanctuary of your soul—a place where peace reigns supreme, and the weary traveler can find rest and rejuvenation. Welcome home to your sanctuary, a realm where the heart is at ease and the spirit dances freely.

## The Future Is Yours to Write: Embracing Uncertainty With Optimism and a Fine Glass of Wine

Ah, the ever-uncertain dance of life! One moment, we're sipping champagne on the deck of certainty, basking in the warm glow of familiar surroundings and predictable outcomes. But oh, how quickly the tide can turn! In the blink of an eye, we find ourselves navigating the choppy seas of unpredictability, tossed about by the waves of change and uncertainty. Yet fear not, my fellow adventurers, for in this vast ocean of unknowns, lies a treasure trove of possibilities waiting to be explored—the future is yours to write, and what better way to embark on this grand adventure than with a fine glass of wine in hand!

Imagine this: you're perched on the edge of tomorrow, uncertainty swirling around you like a tornado of possibilities. The headlines scream with news of economic instability, corporate restructures, and geopolitical upheaval, painting a vivid picture of the turbulent times in which we live. It's enough to make even the bravest souls feel a twinge of apprehension. But amidst the chaos, there is a glimmer of hope—a beacon of light shining through the storm clouds, guiding us toward brighter horizons.

Now, you might be thinking, "But uncertainty is about as comfortable as a cactus hammock!" And you'd be right. We humans have a penchant for seeking comfort in the familiar, craving the security of stable routines and predictable outcomes. We long for the reassuring embrace of stability, the comforting assurance that tomorrow will be just like today, only with fresher donuts and a slightly different shade of blue in the sky.

But here's the thing: life doesn't come with a GPS. There's no roadmap to success, no blueprint for happiness. We're all just winging it, navigating our way through the twists and turns of fate, hoping for the best and praying we don't trip over our own shoelaces in the process. And you know what? That's okay.

Because here's the secret sauce to navigating the murky waters of uncertainty: optimism and a fine glass of wine. Yes, you heard me right. Optimism, that magical elixir that turns lemons into lemonade and setbacks into plot twists. And wine, well, that's just liquid courage in a fancy bottle, emboldening us to face whatever challenges may come our way with grace and resilience.

So, how do we embrace uncertainty like a long-lost friend? By realizing that the unknown isn't the enemy—it's the adventure. Think of life as one big choose-your-own-adventure book, with each twist and turn leading to a new chapter of possibilities. Sure, there might be a few plot twists along the way, but that's what makes the story worth reading. Now, let's take a page out of the playbook of the wise and wily. Whether you're climbing the corporate ladder or building your own empire, success isn't about playing it safe— it's about embracing the unknown like a long-lost friend you never knew you needed.

Take risks, they say. Step out of your comfort zone, they say. And you know what? They're right. Because behind every closed door lies a world of opportunities just waiting to be discovered. Sure, you might stumble. You might fall. But remember, every misstep is just a plot twist in the grand adventure of life.

So, raise your glass to uncertainty, my friends. Toast to the unknown, the unpredictable, and the downright daring. Because in a world where anything is possible, the future is yours to write. And hey, if all else fails, at least you've got a fine glass of wine to drown your sorrows in. Cheers to uncertainty—and may your glass always be half full.

Before we close the chapter, ever wonder why decorators always seem to have a glass of wine in hand while they work? Well, it's not just because they have impeccable taste—it's because they've mastered the art of solo celebrations. You see, for them, every achievement, big or small, is a reason to raise a glass and toast to their success. So, whether you're building a home that reflects your soul or embracing uncertainty with a fine Bordeaux, you can bet there's a celebratory sip involved. Cheers to decorating, one glass at a time!

# Conclusion

In the journey of life, amidst the bustling chaos and cacophony of expectations, this book emerges as a beacon of light, guiding you through the labyrinthine paths of existence with grace, courage, and a touch of indulgence. Through the lens of yoga, reading, sisterhood, and the ever-comforting presence of wine, this book offers not just a manual for survival, but a celebration of the art of living boldly, beautifully, and unapologetically on one's own terms.

At the heart of our quest for inner peace lies the sacred space of the yoga mat—a sanctuary where the chaos of the outside world fades into the background, and we are left alone with our thoughts, our breath, and the gentle rhythm of our bodies. Here, amidst the simplicity of a downward dog or the serenity of a seated meditation, we find solace, strength, and the unwavering certainty that we are enough.

But peace is not merely the absence of turmoil; it is the gentle acceptance of life's ebb and flow, the willingness to embrace both the light and the shadows that dance within us. In the comforting embrace of a well-loved novel or the intoxicating allure of a glass of wine, we find refuge, inspiration, and the courage to face our fears head-on. For in the pages of a book or the depths of a glass, we discover the power of storytelling—the ability to rewrite our own narratives, to dream new dreams, and to find hope in the most unlikely of places.

Yet, amidst the chaos of daily life, we are not alone. Bound by bonds of blood or by the tender threads of friendship, our sisters stand beside us, offering love, support, and a shoulder to lean on when the weight of the world becomes too much to bear. In their laughter, we find solace; in their tears, we find strength; and in their unwavering presence, we find the courage to keep moving forward, one step at a time.

But sisterhood knows no bounds of time or distance. Across the miles, across the years, our connections remain steadfast and true, nurtured by the simple acts of kindness, the shared laughter, and the whispered words of encouragement that bridge the gap between us. Whether through the magic of technology or the timeless beauty of a handwritten letter, we find solace in the knowledge that our sisters are always there, ready to lift us up and remind us of our own strength and resilience.

In the pursuit of happiness, financial independence is a vital cornerstone. Through careful budgeting and mindful spending, we learn to prioritize our needs and desires, finding balance in the delicate dance of saving and splurging. For true wealth lies not in material possessions but in the richness of our experiences—the laughter shared with friends, the quiet moments of solitude, and the simple pleasures that bring joy to our hearts.

As we journey through life, we are guided by the wisdom of those who came before us—the brave, resilient women whose stories inspire us to dream bigger, love harder, and never settle for anything less than we deserve. In their words, we find courage; in their actions, we find hope; and in their unwavering belief in the power of sisterhood, we find the strength to forge our own paths and create our own destinies.

And so, as we raise our glasses to the beauty of life and the strength of sisterhood, let us remember that we are never alone—that in the quiet moments of reflection, in the pages of a beloved book, and in the comforting warmth of a glass of wine, we find solace, inspiration, and the courage to embrace the journey ahead, wherever it may lead.

# About the author

Elizabeth Jane Danin is a woman on a mission to break down barriers and raise the self-esteem of women. After a lifetime of not being single but seeing single friends feeling poorly about themselves, Elizabeth percolated an idea.

What if there was an appropriate book that covered all manner of subjects that were as broad as reading through to budgeting on a single income? Could her own experience bring to bear such a book?

With this in mind, living in Australia and being single (at one stage), income-poor (at another stage), and headstrong and somewhat determined such a mission was courageously taken on and this book came to be.

Elizabeth is fiercely determined that each woman, no matter their circumstances, should feel good about themselves and should not be held back by society's or cultural restraints.

This book was many years in the making, and thus Elizabeth hopes it to be a reference point for years to come.

# Glossary

**Cocktails:** Symbolizing the blending of diverse pleasures and experiences.

**Group chat:** A digital space for shared conversation and support among friends or peers.

**Sassy Guide:** A comprehensive toolkit for nurturing physical, mental, and emotional well-being.

**Home:** A sanctuary for the soul, embodying comfort and belonging.

**Luxury:** Simple indulgences that bring joy and enrichment to life.

**Self-love:** The practice of accepting, valuing, and caring for oneself unconditionally.

**Sisterhood:** Bonds of friendship, support, and solidarity among women.

**Soulmate:** A person who deeply connects with another on a profound emotional and spiritual level.

**Well-being:** Holistic state of health, happiness, and fulfillment.

**Wine:** Catalyst for relaxation, connection, and celebration.

**Wine tasting:** A sensory experience exploring the nuances of different wines, often involving sampling and appreciation.

**Yoga:** Spiritual practice cultivating harmony and inner peace.

# References


Avery, J. (2018, September 24). *10 reasons why women should read romance novels.* Book Riot. https://bookriot.com/why-women-read-romance-novels/

Baxter, R. (n.d.). *Create your own personal sanctuary: Tips for designing the perfect relaxation space!.* Informed Relaxation. https://informedrelaxation.com/create-your-own-personal-sanctuary-tips-for-designing-the-perfect-relaxation-space/

Bejelly, K. (2023, August 10). *Why and how to join a wine club.* A Girl Worth Saving. https://agirlworthsaving.net/wine-club/

Kerry, C. (2023, March 30). *13 easy food and wine pairing ideas everyone should know.* Taste of Home. https://www.tasteofhome.com/collection/food-and-wine-pairing/

Bieber, R. (2021, July 13). *Why I buy used books (and you should too).* Bookstr. https://archive.bookstr.com/article/why-i-buy-used-books-and-you-should-too/

Breyer, M. (2022, September 26). *What a glass of wine a day does to your body.* Verywell Fit. https://www.verywellfit.com/what-glass-wine-day-does-your-body-4864161#:~:text=Drinking%20a%20glass%20of%20wine%20a%20day%20provides,biome%2C%20and%20may%20reduce%20the%20likelihood%20of%20gallstones.

Chandler, V. (2017, May 24). *When actually is 'wine o'clock'?.* Good Housekeeping. https://www.goodhousekeeping.com/uk/food/a569016/best-time-drink-wine/

Collins, H. (2023, May 22). *7 financial planning strategies for single women.* Smart Asset. https://smartasset.com/financial-advisor/financial-planning-for-single-women

Connors, C.D. (2018, November 16). *The feeling of achievement - 10 ways to celebrate success improves your life.* Medium. https://medium.com/the-mission/the-feeling-of-achievement-10-ways-celebrating-success-improves-your-life-41532a964ff3

*Cooking for one: The ultimate solo kitchen guide.* (2023, May 30). The Solo Spoon. https://www.thesolospoon.com/cooking-for-one-guide/

Cronkleton, E. (2023, May26). *Yoga for anxiety: 11 poses to try.* Healthline. https://www.healthline.com/health/anxiety/yoga-for-anxiety#hero-pose

Dunn, E. & Courtney, C. (2020, September 14). *Does more money make us more happy?*. Harvard Business Review. https://hbr.org/2020/09/does-more-money-really-makes-us-more-happy

Dutt, S.S. (2016, June 20). *Downward facing dog: Exploration, anatomy, and alignment*. Yoga with Sapna. https://yogawithsapna.com/downward-facing-dog-exploration-anatomy-and-alignment/

*11 benefits of yoga for women to support health and wellbeing*. (2023, October). Calm. https://blog.calm.com/blog/benefits-of-yoga-for-women#:~:text=11%20benefits%20of%20yoga%20for%20women%20to%20support,women%20FAQs%20...%204%20Calm%20your%20mind.%20

*Embracing the single journey: Navigating the ups and downs of singlehood*. (2024, March 8). LinkedIn: Life Solutions Investments (Pty) Ltd T/A EM Training & Consultancy. https://www.linkedin.com/pulse/embracing-single-journey-navigating-ups-downs-singlehood-xuwpf/

*From friends to sisters: A heartwarming story of friendship turned into sisterhood [5 tips to strengthen your bonds]*. (2023, April 16). Emerg Woman Magazine. https://emergewomanmagazine.com/from-friends-to-sisters-a-heartwarming-story-of-friendship-turned-into-sisterhood-5-tips-to-strengthen-your-bonds/

Gillingham, K. & Rusciano, A. (2023, December 9). *How to choose a good book*. Wiki How. https://www.wikihow.com/Choose-a-Good-Book#:~:text=Things%20You%20Should%20Know%201%20Pick%20a%20book,BookRiot%20to%20find%20book%20lists%20for%20all%20preferences.

Gobler, E. (2023, May 25). *How to live a luxurious lifestyle on a budget*. Clever Girl Finance. https://www.clevergirlfinance.com/live-a-luxurious-lifestyle-on-a-budget/

Hagan, E. (2022, March 16). *The mental health benefits of reading*. Psychology Today. https://www.psychologytoday.com/us/blog/the-art-effect/202203/the-mental-health-benefits-reading

Hall, L. (2021, May 19). *Tips to reduce food waste in the solo kitchen*. Solo Living. https://wearesololiving.com/tips-reducing-food-waste-in-the-solo-kitchen/

Hammond, J. (2019, May 13). *11 cocktails from around the world you need to try*. Culture Trip. https://theculturetrip.com/north-america/usa/articles/11-signature-cocktails-around-world

Hardin, B. (2020, September 1). *Wine 101: Types of wine $ basics for beginners*. The Cookiee Rookie. https://www.thecookierookie.com/wine-101-types-of-wines-beginners/

*How to setup wine & food pairings at home.* (n.d.). Triwine. https://triwineapp.com/how-to-setup-wine-food-pairings-at-home/

Johnson, A. (2022, January 24). *9 benefits of a book club (and why you should join one!).* Bonafide Bookworm. https://bonafidebookworm.com/benefits-of-a-book-club/

Johnson, C. (2019, December 9). *The connection between feeling good and looking good.* Thrive Global. https://community.thriveglobal.com/the-connection-between-feeling-good-and-looking-good/

Johnson, C. (2021, January 17). *Mindful breathing.* Anahana. https://www.anahana.com/en/breathing-exercise/mindful-breathing#:~:text=Improved%20anxiety%20management%20Improved%20sleep%20Pain%20management%20Decreased,lowers%20heart%20rate%2C%20and%20calms%20the%20nervous%20system.

Kropf, J. (2024, February 26). *25 best ways: How to invest in yourself as a woman (2024).* Wealthy Woman Finance. https://wealthywomanfinance.com/invest-yourself-woman/

McCaffrey, K. (2022, December 19). *12 ways to use leftovers in your weekly meal plan.* Slender Kitchen. https://www.slenderkitchen.com/article/12-ways-to-use-leftovers-in-your-weekly-meal-plan

Mccleland, L. (2019, September 10). *Taking your workout look from studio to street.* Vie Active. https://vieactivewear.com/blogs/news/taking-your-workout-look-from-studio-to-street

Murphy, L. (n.d.). *Why I'm obsessed with reading romance novels: 20 reasons why you should too.* She Reads Romance Books. https://www.shereadsromancebooks.com/why-you-should-read-romance-novels/

Mushayamunda, F. (2023, March 6). *50 powerful women empowerment quotes that'll leave you inspired.* Today. https://www.today.com/life/quotes/women-empowerment-quotes-rcna42474

Oliveri, K. (2021, April 23). *5 yummy food & wine pairings to practice at home.* Wine Traveler. https://www.winetraveler.com/wine-pairing/5-great-food-wine-pairing-recipes-at-home/

*Poems about pain.* (n.d.). All Poetry. https://allpoetry.com/poems/about/Pain

Rice, A. (2021, October 26). *Yoga for anxiety: 9 poses to try.* Psych Central. https://psychcentral.com/anxiety/yoga-for-anxiety#is-it-effective

Russell, T. (2021, September 27). *How to sharpen your swords with Yoga's warrior pose.* Greatist. https://greatist.com/fitness/warrior-pose#what-is-warrior-pose

Sanjana. (2023, June 1). *The single ladies guide to handling finances.* Women Who Money. https://womenwhomoney.com/single-ladies-guide-to-managing-finances/

Shrestha, S. (2019, March 27). *Read. Reflect. Repeat. How taking reading and reflection hand-in-hand enhanced my reading experience!* Medium. https://medium.com/@sthashraddha/read-reflect-repeat-a7d4e36of623

*6 Ways to Maintain Long-distance Friendships for a Lifetime.* (2023, March 26). Utopia. https://utopia.org/guide/long-distance-friendship-maintaining-relationships-from-afar/#:~:text=Send%20photos%20regularly%2C%20write%20to%20your%20long-distance%20friends,little%20things%20that%20count.%20Create%20routines%20and%20rituals.

Suri, K. (2020, January 29). *Pranayama: The science of breathing (full guide).* The Yogi Press. https://www.yogi.press/home/pranayama-a-full-guide

Tegtman, J. (2021, August 30). *Pairing books and wine.* Read More Co. https://www.readmoreco.com/blogs/book-news/pairing-books-and-wines

*Twelve tips for single women to thrive and achieve success.* (2023, April 2). Medium. https://medium.com/hello-love/12-tips-for-single-women-to-thrive-and-achieve-success-eccbb3090983

Twomey, A. (2020, December 10). *Women writing about women: Must-read memoirs, biographies, and autobiographies. https://bookriot.com/memoirs-biographies-and-autobiographies-by-and-about-women/*

Warrell, M. (2015, July 21). *Why embracing uncertainty is critical to your success.* Forbes. https://www.forbes.com/sites/margiewarrell/2015/07/21/why-embracing-uncertainty-is-critical-to-your-success/?sh=577a34ac673c

*Why you should borrow books.* (2021, July 21). Aslan's Library. https://aslanslibrary.wordpress.com/2010/07/21/why-you-should-borrow-books/

Zipperlen, C. (2023, October 9). *Every curve: A comprehensive guide to embracing body positivity for women.* Ananda Soul. https://anandasoul.com/blogs/blog/embracing-body-positivity-women